what is
a spiritual
Master?

Omraam Mikhaël Aïvanhov

what is
a spiritual
Master?

Translated from the French
2nd edition

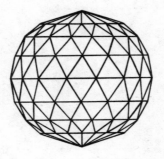

Collection Izvor
No. 207

EDITIONS PROSVETA

By the same author:
(translated from the French)

Izvor Collection

© 1984 by Prosveta S.A. – B.P. 12 – F-83601 Fréjus
ALL RIGHTS RESERVED

ISBN 2-85566-300-8
1ère édition : ISBN 2-85566-230-3
édition originale : ISBN 2-85566-193-5

TABLE OF CONTENTS

EDITOR'S NOTE

The reader is asked to bear in mind that the Editors have retained the spoken style of the Master Omraam Mikhaël Aïvanhov in his presentation of the Teaching of the great Universal White Brotherhood, the essence of the Teaching being the spoken Word.

They also wish to clarify the point that the word *white* in Universal White Brotherhood does not refer to colour or race, but to purity of soul. The Teaching shows how all men without exception (universal), can live a new form of life on earth (brotherhood), in harmony (white) and with respect for each other's race, creed and country... that is, Universal White Brotherhood.

1

HOW TO RECOGNIZE
A TRUE SPIRITUAL MASTER

A disciple who has met his Master has found a mother who will carry him in her womb for nine months so that he may be born into the spiritual world. Once he has been born, once his consciousness has awakened, his eyes will discover the beauty of creation, his ears will hear divine words, he will taste heavenly food, his feet will bear him throughout space on errands of good and his hands will learn to create in the finer, higher worlds of the soul.

Very few people understand what a Master really is. They have read books which tell all sorts of unlikely tales: a Master is perfect, all knowing, and all powerful; he has no need to eat, drink or sleep; he is beyond temptation and above all, he spends his time performing miracles. All these ideas can be found in Spalding's "The Life of Masters," and many people have been swept off their feet by this book, never questioning the improbability of many of the anecdotes. Great Masters have indeed got exceptional powers, but they never use them for performing feats to astound the casual bystander. Even though they are capable of appearing and disappearing, of walking on water, flying through the air, producing banquets, passing unhurt through flames or raising houses out of the dust, true Masters will not do these things, as to witness such happenings does not help people to work on themselves and change.

It is important you know that a Master is made exactly like all other men: he has the same organs, he feels the same needs and has the same longings. If you cut him, his blood will flow red like everybody else's. What makes him different is that his consciousness is very much greater than that of most people: the Master has an ideal, he sees things from a higher point of view and above all, he has achieved perfect control over himself. Clearly, it takes an enormous amount of time and work to achieve this, and that is why no one can become a Master in a single incarnation.

Should you meet a Master, you must realize that all the qualities and virtues that he manifests have not been acquired in just this one lifetime. He will have had to have worked over centuries, even millennia, and the qualities that he has gained by his own work not only remain with him when he leaves the earth but return with him too. So from incarnation to incarnation he keeps adding new spiritual elements to his being until the day comes when he can truly conduct light and heavenly virtues.

Unfortunately, there are also those who have been working over the centuries to become conductors of hellish forces and they are masters of black magic. People are free to choose either good or evil. Should they choose evil, Cosmic Intelligence will let them continue on this path a certain time, according to the degree of their revolt against the universal order, but they will always finish by being annihilated. At the beginning, however, man has a free choice. As long as he is alive, he is free to choose which direction his path should take.

Very occasionally, under rare circumstances, you can find beings whose path is fixed, despite the free will which is given them. Great Initiates, for example, are pre-determined for light and for love. Some of them may have indeed fallen, but the majority have remained spirits of light. Moreover, as time goes on, it becomes less possible for them to change direction: through their work they succeed in so spiritualizing their physical material that they become untarnishable, like pure gold. Until a being has arrived at this degree of evolution, it is always possible for him to change direction and you can find cases in history of white magicians who have become black magicians.

If you are wondering what one has to do to become a black magician, I will tell you that in fact it is very simple, so simple that even you can become one. All you have to do is to give way to your lower nature. If you keep on breaking the laws of goodness, justice and love through trying to be successful at the expense of others, if you push people around and destroy them, then you, too, will be on the way to becoming a black magician. There it is, clear and simple. Many imagine that you have to have a diabolical master who will teach you all sorts of wicked incantations and the art of casting magical spells. Of course this can happen, but you do not have to have a master to work for evil; even without any teacher, any magical formulas, anything, you can become a black magician merely by letting yourself be too much influenced by your lower nature. The same goes for those who think only of helping and enlightening others: even if they have no Master teaching them, they are on their way to becoming a white magician.

In fact, everybody has a master, whether visible or invisible. Criminals have masters in the invisible world who keep on suggesting that they should harm others. They may well say, "What, us? A Master? Not on your life!" but these blind people should realize that they do have a master and that they follow his pernicious advice, day and night.

Obviously, when I talk to you of the Masters, I always mean the great spiritual Masters, the true white magicians. I know very well that the title of Master is given to many craftsmen to show that they excel in their work, and that lawyers, magistrates and artists are also given this name. It is a way of looking at things, and I would not deny them their title. However, you must understand that a true Master, in the spiritual meaning of the term, is a being who first of all knows the essential verities, not what people have written, invented or told in legend, but the essential truths as seen by Cosmic Intelligence. Secondly, a true Master has to have both the will and the ability to dominate, master and control everything within him. Finally, this science and this control which he has acquired must only be used to manifest all the qualities and virtues of unselfish love.

A true Master is recognized by his disinterestedness. Every Master who comes on earth has a particular quality to manifest: there are, therefore, Masters of wisdom or of strength or of purity... but all of them, without exception, have in common this quality of disinterestedness.

There are so many impostors and charlatans, ready to take advantage of people's naïvety! They merely read a few old books on occult science (often written by ignorant people) and with no more ado, they parade themselves as great Masters. There are no signs on them that Heaven has acknowledged them, they just call themselves Masters and think that that is enough. As for their followers, instead of studying their leader a while to see how he behaves, they follow him with their eyes closed. They will be deceived, stripped of everything and enslaved, but they will not even notice. What a magnificent state of affairs! You can at least say that the so-called Master is a pretty shrewd human being whereas his followers are fools. Why not ask where he has come from, how he has lived, who his Master was and who sent him? No, they do not see the point of such questions; as they have been promised initiation in three days (at the cost of a few thousand dollars, to be sure!), they will believe him. You see they are in a hurry, and so their initiation must not take longer than three days! The world is full of people like that, humbugs and swindlers who demonstrate their own intelligence by taking advantage of the credulity and the stupidity of others.

I do not deny that these people have certain powers – anybody who does certain exercises can get powers – but the question is to know how to use them and to what end, because it is on this that Heaven judges us. Heaven is not concerned with the abilities we have but with the use we make of them; not with our knowledge, our clairvoyance or powers, but with our disinterestedness. You can have all the knowledge, clairvoyance and powers in the world; but if you are not disinterested, even though people regard you as a Master, Heaven will not acknowledge you.

The real tragedy is people's lack of discernment: should they meet a true Master who is totally disinterested, they are wary of him, whereas the first person who turns up and throws dust into their eyes by saying that he is a Master, will be followed. In fact, a true Master will never once say that he is a Master but rather he will let you feel it and understand it. He is in no hurry to be recognized. However, once a false Master has decreed that he is a Master, he will only be concerned with imposing his will on others.

I have just received a letter from a man who thinks he is capable of being a spiritual guide, yet he wrote to me of his difficulties and sufferings. How can he deceive people by pretending to guide them whilst he himself is still confused? Obviously it would be better if he waited. Who told him to take on this task? People believe that they are capable of guiding others before they have gained the necessary virtues of wisdom, love, purity, strength and unselfishness and that is not the way things should be at all. Until you have received the order from a higher being that you should take on this crushing task of directing and guiding people, it is very dangerous to want to play this role.

I would very much like to help this particular man, because I can see that he is very unhappy and that he does not even know the reason for his unhappiness. He thought it was enough to read a few books of occult knowledge and then invoke the mighty powers of the invisible world, making use of them without ever having learnt that the first thing he must do is to get himself into harmony with them. Naturally, these forces take their revenge, "Why are you trying to make use of us just to satisfy your own whims? You are weak, ignorant and we do not wish to submit to you. In fact, you deserve a good lesson." There are many so-called occultists who have no real knowledge of the laws of the spiritual world. I repeat, they have read a few books and, without having prepared themselves at all, they want to flabbergast their disciples by performing marvels. Oh no, this is no way to set about things.

If you are to assume the role of spiritual

guide, you must first have received a diploma. The diplomas which exist on the physical plane also have their counterparts above, awarded in just the same way. Luminous spirits, who have sent us to earth, watch us, measure us and if they see that we have made efforts and that we have succeeded in dominating ourselves and correcting some of our faults, they give us a diploma. What kind of diploma? Certainly not a paper which could be obliterated or destroyed but, instead, our faces are stamped with a mark, as are our bodies, in proof that we have achieved a victory over ourselves. People may perhaps not see it, but all the luminous spirits of nature see it from afar and obey us and come to help us.

Yes indeed, in order to have the right to carry out certain tasks on the spiritual plane, we must also obtain the approval of certain beings and, believe me, that approval is not easily given. Many who have wanted to become teachers or professors found that the studies they had to undergo were long and difficult, but those studies are nothing, nothing at all, when compared to the conditions that have to be fulfilled by those who want to teach their disciples the truths of Initiatic Science. I am always amazed by the ignorance and naïvety of people on this question : just about anybody thinks he is qualified to use the title of Master and when most people meet a true Master, they think that he has fallen straight from Heaven just like that, perfect, and without ever having had to put in any work!

You will never find any being who has come to earth perfect. Whether he shows it or not, everyone has at least one weakness, if not several. Even the great Initiates have weaknesses: it may be fear, or pride, or greed or sensuality. The superiority of an Initiate lies in the fact that, first of all, he is aware of his weakness and then that he uses all means to triumph over it.

When a being comes to incarnate on this earth, however elevated his spirit may be, he will inherit from his parents a more-or-less defective matter which he has to transform. This he does by using his other qualities and virtues and so he becomes even greater after this success because he has managed to transform crude material into a more refined material which can be used in his work. One can really discover the power of the spirit with Initiates for they have learnt to dominate everything, whereas most people drag behind them weaknesses they have not been able to conquer throughout their whole life.

You must understand that an Initiate comes to earth bearing those qualities which he has worked on in previous incarnations; because of these qualities he instinctively avoids the evil path and directs himself towards constructive and luminous activities. Even if he can remember nothing, he is pushed, despite himself, to continue in the same direction that he held in the past. I had absolutely no memory of my previous incarnations for many years, but I came to this life with certain traces stamped on me which pushed me in a particular direction.

I know very well that some of you will be astounded and shocked to hear that even great Masters do not arrive on this earth perfect. I hope Christians will forgive me when I say that Jesus himself was not perfect: he, too, had to learn, to study, to improve himself and to do a great work of purification before he received the Holy Spirit when he was thirty. Unfortunately the Gospels do not tell us what he did in that period between twelve and thirty. Without exception, every being who comes into this world receives worn-out and tarnished particles with which to form his body and so these particles must be purified, ordered and harmonized. How could this material which has been handed down from generation to generation over the centuries have stayed pure and unblemished? Even an Initiate who has been born to exceptional parents has to do a mighty work on his physical body so that it may become the perfect instrument for his spirit. Perhaps this Initiate may be destined to bring a new religion but, even so, he has to re-

lease his spirit from the grip of matter by transforming, spiritualizing and sublimating it. Heav-
en will measure his greatness according to the
length of time he takes to achieve it.

Even Jesus was not immediately able to manifest the power of his spirit. First of all he had to
study, to exercise himself and then, at last, in his
thirtieth year, he began to perform miracles.
The lives of all great spiritual Masters begin with
a long period in which they are ignorant of their
mission. Even if, in their youth, they receive certain revelations from the divine world, they have
no idea of their real greatness. I know that many
people will refuse to believe such a thing : they
prefer to think that an Initiate arrives on earth
omniscient and all powerful. This is not the case
at all ; some of them even have physical and psychic weaknesses which they never manage to
overcome. It would take too long to go into all
the details, but if I did, you would discover
many extremely interesting things.

Do you think that when I was young I was as
I am today ? I, too, have had to work years and
years on myself and there is nothing more difficult than that. The soul and the spirit are of divine essence and they can be seen and understood as such in their world, but they must also
be seen and understood through matter, through
the physical body. This is the greatest mystery of

existence which is symbolized in the image of the snake swallowing its tail. The head of the snake represents the spirit, the Higher Self, and it has to manifest itself through the tail, through matter, or the lower self. Spirit, which is all knowing and all powerful on high, has to look at itself through the mirror of matter. The goal of Initiation is so to transform matter that it can reflect back the spirit's own true likeness.

We have come back, as always, to this work that has to be done on matter: that is the true mission of us all on this earth. You must not imagine life to be easy, even for the great Masters. In fact it is quite the opposite, for they are the ones to encounter the greatest difficulties. Precisely because they have both the means and the will to do the work, they are granted the heaviest of tasks, both within themselves and in their surrounding circumstances and, through these difficulties, they become even greater. Yes, because of these difficulties.

The true greatness of an Initiate, of a Master, lies in his ability to come to earth, face the same tests as everyone else but yet to manage, little by little, to raise himself above them all. Only when he has done that, has he the right to instruct others and even to shake them up. By conquering his weaknesses, he has acquired the right to guide people as this is the one and only condition which allows anyone the right to open his mouth and to teach others. If he has not got rid of his own faults and yet wants to meddle in others' affairs, it would be better for him to keep quiet, otherwise not only will people sense something a bit suspicious about him, but circumstances themselves will set a few traps for him. How do you think you can convince someone of the need to get rid of a weakness when you still have it yourself? How can a coward give courage to others? If he is shouting, "Forward!" whilst his knees are knocking together in terror, how will he be able to encourage the crowd to follow him? Understand that only victory over your own weaknesses will give you real powers, and that, sooner or later, these powers will shine through your eyes, your gestures, your face and your voice. They will manifest even if you wish to hide them.

A Master who has worked over thousands of years to conquer all his human passions and to attract all the virtues of Heaven, emanates beneficial elements for those who are around him. The usefulness of a Master lies in the fact that by listening to him, looking at him and living close to him, his disciples receive some particles of his life which allow them to evolve much more quickly. Otherwise, what do you think is the use of a Master to you? He is not concerned with giving you riches or a job or women; his sole care is to give you elements of a higher nature which vibrate in harmony with Heaven. If you can receive these elements, if you can keep them and even make them grow, you will find that in time, your thoughts, feelings and even your health will improve. You find nothing but blessings near a true Master.

2

THE NECESSITY
FOR A SPIRITUAL MASTER

If you want to learn the violin, you buy an instrument and books of exercises and start practising. For the first few days, you work for an hour or two each day, but very quickly the first enthusiasm wanes and you abandon your instrument. A week later, you again turn to your violin for a while and then, once again, you give up.... So the time passes; sometimes you feel very keen and, at others, you feel lazy and so your work alternates according to your feelings. However, if you have a teacher, you want to win his approval and respect and so you work steadily to prepare for the day of your lesson. The teacher corrects your mistakes, encourages you and under his guidance, you end up by being a virtuoso. You never hear of any great musician who has reached the top of his profession without having had a teacher.

The same thing applies in the spiritual world. If you do not have a Master, it is very difficult for you to keep persevering. You think that it would be good for you to meditate and make efforts to improve, but very quickly your old habits creep in. A few months later, you remember all your good intentions, and once again you start trying... until the day when you finally fall back into inertia. However, if you have a Master, you feel continuously stimulated; he draws you along both by his words and his example. He touches your feelings and because you love and admire him, you are pushed to work on transforming yourself.

Of course, this does not stop you from falling back into your old mistakes but, each time, you remake your good resolutions and one day, the strength produced by these resolutions will be triumphant. The most serious thing is not to lapse into mistakes, but to give up hope that you will ever conquer them and thereby relinquish any effort to change yourself. You must really understand the power of a decision. From the day you sincerely decide to change because your Master has shown you the dangers of the path you are on, this decision is recorded and makes a new point of departure within. Even if you see no immediate results, that recorded decision will give results one day. Herein lies the usefulness of a Master.

Above all, I want to make you understand that given the nature of the spiritual world, it would be better not to penetrate it at all than to penetrate it without a guide. Some have found this out to their cost; they bought books which gave them techniques of concentration, meditation or respiration and they flung themselves into these exercises and became physically and psychically unbalanced. It would have been better for these people if they had been less persevering!

I am always amazed by the fact that those who would never dream of climbing a mountain without a guide leap, without a moment's thought, into exploring the psychic world on their own. The dangers of that world are much greater than merely getting lost, falling into abysses or being engulfed by avalanches and yet they think that they can manage perfectly well. This, of course, is the reason why there are so many unbalanced people amongst so-called spiritualists. They leapt in without any guide and so were lost....

None of these disagreeable things need have happened if the spiritualists had been aware, right from the beginning, of one essential thing: the work can only be undertaken safely by those who have first prepared and practised the qualities and virtues of love, gentleness, purity and submission to the divine world... because willpower is not enough in this world.

Many spiritualists make the mistake of not having a solid enough base for their activities. They leap in without any preparation, thinking that all that is necessary is to desire that the invisible world should reveal itself to them and that angels will then come to serve them and all powers will fall into their hands. Oh no, unfortunately it is not like that at all. The true spiritualist spends twenty or thirty years under the direction of a Master, preparing himself, and then, after that, he can obtain all he wants in a very short time. It is the preparation which takes all the time in the spiritual domain. However, people do not prepare themselves, they go on harbouring all sorts of bizarre thoughts and are unconcerned about the filth and injustice within them. From time to time, of course, they do a little of what they call meditation and think that that is enough. Perhaps it is enough for them, but in reality it is not enough at all. There are certain preliminary conditions that have to be fulfilled, even for meditation.

Nowadays meditation is all the rage and more and more people claim that they meditate. They gain nothing from their meditation, however, because meditation cannot be done, just like that, without preparation.... How can anyone meditate who has never had a high ideal, who has never given up any of his pleasures, his disorderly living, his desires, his wine and tobacco? He says he meditates, but what does he meditate on? His topics are money, power, or someone that he wants to seduce. How can you meditate on heavenly subjects when you have no high ideal which will lift you above an ordinary life, a mere animal existence, all the way to Heaven? It is impossible to meditate if you have not first conquered certain weaknesses and understood certain truths. Furthermore, not only can you not meditate but it is even dangerous for you to try.

The most remarkable aspect of inner work is that there is no exercise of thought which does not have results. There are always results, only unfortunately sometimes they are deplorable. Why? Because man does not know how to raise himself higher to find light on the mental plane, he merely moves around elements in his inner world without purifying or organizing them; he stirs up all that is foggy, murky and twilit; he has only stayed in the marshes of the astral plane.

The most important thing, therefore, is to find a Master who will give you the best ways to work so that you can advance in the spiritual life. The best methods are those that are the least dangerous and the most efficacious; they may take longer, but they will be the most durable.

Unfortunately, though, people are in such a
hurry that they do not have the time, patience or
confidence to commit themselves to a luminous
path which, though slower, is more sure. They
think that they can become mediums, magicians
or clairvoyants in the same way that you can become a pedicurist or a manicurist and as soon as
they obtain a little success, they make a great
production out of it. In this way, they mislead
many people as the majority of humanity has no
criteria and so swallows everything it is offered.

The essential thing is not intelligence, riches
and power, but to be well-directed, because then
you can be sure of success. If you are not well
guided, however, even if you possess all sorts of
qualities – power, intelligence, goodness, you
will always run the risk of falling flat on your
face.

3

THE SORCERER'S APPRENTICE

Jesus said, "Neither cast ye your pearls before swine." The pearls he was speaking of are great initiatic truths; not everybody is ready yet to accept them, and if you give them to some people they will not only not appreciate them, but will turn and tear you apart. So you see, it is a very risky business to reveal spiritual truths to those who are not ready to receive them. All Initiates and great Masters are obliged to think about the consequences of the revelations which they wish to make because although a truth can illumine some, it can also provoke dangerous fermentations in others.

The quintessence of ancient Initiations is contained in the four commands – "know," "want," "dare," and "be silent." Why is the last one, "to be silent," necessary? The discoveries made by the preceding three activities of "learning," "wanting" and "daring" are of such power that it is very dangerous to reveal them to those who are either not ready to receive them or who have evil intentions. So silence is necessary and shows the immeasurable importance of this knowledge, this desire and this daring. One of the greatest tragedies of mankind is its tendency to use the best things for the worst enterprises. Things which should be for salvation are used for ruin. Many seekers have regretted their discoveries which were immediately used by others in a destructive way. In the future it will be different; the command will be, "Know, want, dare and then speak out!" As people become more highly evolved, they can be given the greatest revelations which will then produce magnificent effects. However, until this time comes, you must keep quiet and follow the advice of Jesus not to cast your pearls before swine

You object, "One cannot leave people floundering in the dark!" Of course not, but you must know that all the secrets of Initiatic Science can become very dangerous weapons in the hands of egotistical people. The selfish and the cruel will only make use of them for their own good and to the detriment of others. Look at what occurs today. Many books are published which reveal the power of thought and its ability to influence people and even to move objects. People form groups and practise with this power so that they can, for example, influence the athletes in the

Olympic games in order that some win and others lose. This is straightforward black magic. We have no right to use the power of thought for such purposes.

As soon as new discoveries appear, there are always all sorts of people without either morality or conscience who want to make use of them in order to impose their crushing will on others. Man's prehistoric nature pushes him to use anything that falls into his hands to make sure that he is the one to end up on top. Man's first inspiration is not to do good but always to do evil. So I am under no illusions : modern interest and curiosity in occult sciences does not indicate progress along the path of spirituality. Quite the contrary, for many it is a descent into black magic.

Not long ago, I received a man of about thirty who wanted me to free him from a spell. It appeared that a woman, much older than him, had cast a spell upon him ; none of the people he had been to see had been able to help him and finally someone suggested that he should try me. I began by asking him some questions about his activities and his studies. He told me that he was an alchemist, that he knew everything, that he had nothing more to learn and that he had even found the philosopher's stone. He showed me a small amount of black powder in a black glass jar. I said, "The philosopher's stone is red. What on earth is that?" "Oh," he replied, "it can turn a little red!" I was amazed by his lack of awareness and said to him, "Listen, if you had really found the philosopher's stone, you would not be in the state you are in now, searching for someone to remove a spell from you. In fact, you have no real knowledge, you buried yourself in books which you do not even understand; you have played with fire and now this is the result of it all."

I met so many people in Paris whose only interest was in the occult arts. They were so proud to be regarded as astrologists, alchemists and kabbalists, without realizing that their whole existence was in total, horrific chaos. For this reason, were I to give one piece of advice to the world, it would be, "Leave the occult arts alone!" You have to manifest your knowledge in your daily living; it comes out in your attitude and in your behaviour. True knowledge is knowing how to dominate yourself, how to free yourself from certain weaknesses so that you are not always at the mercy of inner arguments.

If you could only have seen this boy's eyes and seen how his face looked... I was so sorry for him! I could, however, do nothing for him. If someone has not decided to make an effort himself, it is absolutely useless for anyone else, even the greatest of Masters, to try to free him. I said this to him. I also said, "You claim that you have been put under a spell to justify your present state. No, it was you who put yourself into this dreadful situation because you love your chaotic universe. Therefore, it is you and you alone who can do something about getting yourself out of this mess. All I can do is to give you a philosophy which will help you; you will find it in my books. Go and read them, think about them and when you can see more clearly, come back to me. At the moment, there is no point in us talking further."

Some of you will find my attitude cruel. It is not cruel at all. It is up to him, first of all, to decide to put order back within himself. A Master is not there to give his time and energy to people who have decided that they are great Initiates whilst still leading disorderly lives and who do not have the slightest desire to do any inner work of cleaning up and putting things in order. These people are the first victims of their position and of the evil entities that they have thus attracted. There are thousands of such people in the world. What would happen if they all came here because they had heard that they could meet someone who would free them without their having to make the slightest effort? The Bonfin must not become a psychiatric hospital!

My work is not with the mentally ill. There are others who can, and who do, do this work.

However, to return to this young man, I want to insist, once again, on the great dangers which await most people if they meddle prematurely with the occult arts. In the future, I think we will be able to create specialized sections here and each person will choose the discipline which attracts him most, whether it be alchemy, magic, astrology, clairvoyance, magnetism or being mediumistic. However, that time has not yet come. Before you plunge into all these fields, the first step is to learn how to eat, to breathe, to love, to think, to act and then after that, knowledge will come, an immense and infinite science. The most important thing is to learn to live properly so that you can become stronger. Even knowledge is dangerous, if you have not developed certain qualities which allow you to make right use of it.

For example, people want to know about their previous lives. Of course, this can help them understand certain events in their present existence; but why do you think that Cosmic Intelligence has left a veil over people's memories, had it been really useful for them to remember their previous lives? If it were really necessary, there would have been no veil and everybody would remember. Do you want to know what would happen if, things being as they are now, people could remember their previous lives? As they have not worked on the qualities of pity, tolerance and generosity, when they discovered that somebody had harmed them, robbed them or even murdered them, you can imagine how things would turn out! Once again, there would be endless rows and brawls.... Whereas if they remember nothing, if they do not know that the man who was their greatest enemy in a previous incarnation is now a member of their family, (which often happens), everything will go well and this very ignorance will help them to put their affairs right more easily.

Knowledge is often dangerous. The only really useful knowledge for you is that which allows you to discover the laws of life without leading you into other temptations which may hinder your evolution. Many people want to be clairvoyant, but clairvoyance is one of the most terrible of gifts should you develop it prematurely. All you will see will be the horrifying realities of the astral world, and you will suffer so much that you may even ask the Lord to take the gift away from you. As long as you are not sufficiently developed to be capable of lifting yourself up to contemplate the divine world, you will always be an unhappy victim. It is hideous to be able to look at all that goes on in the hearts and minds of people. It is not enough to be able to see, you must also be capable of standing up to what you see. You must become stronger and purify yourself; these are the only conditions under which you can develop clairvoyance without danger, because then you will even have powers over evil spirits.

I know that many of you wish that I dwelt much more on the practise of occult arts but you do not realize that you are desiring things which are not only not very useful but which can even also be poisonous for you. Trust me and realize that I know what I am doing. I have a programme and everything is unfolding according to this programme. You see, people are like children, in that they are always attracted to what will injure them or make them ill. Under the influence of some book, they decide to throw themselves into those experiences without knowing the dangers. To be protected from these dangers you must be guided by very elevated entities and these entities will not agree to guide you unless they see that you have done an inner work of purification and that you are also disinterested. They are not going to bother themselves with the first greedy fool who comes along wanting to use the powers of the invisible world merely in order to satisfy his whims.

Most of the people I have met (and God

knows I have met them!) show by their attitude, their remarks, their implications and mental reservations that they are interested only in power. Nobody is interested in goodness, love and purity as there are no material advantages to be gained from them. However, it is precisely these virtues which will protect you from all dangers and will shower blessings upon you. Most people do not see this and even if it is explained, they do not want to admit it. In any case, I warn you, do not expect anything other from me than my insistence on these virtues. Even if they are not considered as advantageous, it does not matter; we will go on working over the years on these useless and uninteresting virtues, leaving unexplored all those beautiful and tempting things which occult science has to offer... and one day you will see who is right.

I have met many mediums who were in a deplorable state because they had no way of defending themselves against the spirits of the invisible world. It is marvellous to be sensitive, but if you have not developed your willpower, if you have not learnt how to become resistant, you are lost. In order to be able to predict things they want, as it were, to abandon themselves to the spirits, but, you know, there are all sorts of spirits. Some of them, seeing these people are without any protection, make use of them, deceive

them and absorb all their strength. In a few
years, you will find these poor people completely unbalanced; whether in one area or in another, they will have gone downhill; they will
have begun to drink, to have hallucinations, to
give themselves up to debauchery or they will
have lost their health.... Before leaping into any
experiences, you must know what the dangers
are. It is not good enough merely to be attracted
by certain aspects of the occult arts. All true
Masters will tell you that. However, the day they
see that you are ready, they themselves will tear
off the veils and all you want to see and know
will be accessible, there before your eyes.

Some people for example have heard about
the force of Kundalini which yogis in India have
learnt to awaken. Immediately, without knowing all the preliminary work of purification
which has gone on before awakening this force,
they decide that they, too, are going to arouse it.
What are they going to do with this Kundalini
once they have awakened it? They are going to
be burnt by it, that's all! I had this experience
when I was very young; I was seventeen and I
had been doing breathing exercises for days on
end, and one day, all of a sudden, Kundalini
awoke. It was a terrible sensation, as if my head
was on fire; I was very afraid. I then made gigantic efforts to make it go to sleep again – yes, such

efforts; and I succeeded. Kundalini can even wake in those who are not very spiritually advanced; it can also be awakened accidentally, and as it is a terrible force, those who are not ready for it can become mad or be led right to Hell. What happened to me when I was young could have been the greatest disaster for me if I had not been capable of making this force go to sleep once again. Fortunately, Heaven was watching over me.

Therefore, my dear brothers and sisters, do not rush into experiences in the occult sciences. First of all begin by linking yourself to purity and light and then one day, all spiritual realizations will be possible for you.

4

THE EXOTIC
SHOULD NOT BE CONFUSED
WITH SPIRITUALITY

I

More and more Western countries are being invaded by teachings which come from the East. I am not denying the value of these age-old teachings and disciplines. All the great religions and philosophies of India, Tibet, China and Japan have been the highest peaks of spiritual thought. What I do question, however, is the efficacy of these "yogas" for the West, particularly in view of the way they are practised, even if Indians, Tibetans and Japanese should come to teach them. I see that for the majority it all stays external and superficial. How can people imagine that the practice of a few *asanas* (attitudes, postures), *moudras* (gestures) and the recital of a few mantras will transform you? People will say that these were the postures Buddha adopted when he meditated under his fig tree and that he received illumination. I agree that this may be so, but first of all, we must take into consideration what state Buddha was in. It was not his postures and gestures that made him Buddha; it was his exceptional qualities; whatever position he had taken, these qualities would have still manifested.

I am not saying that certain postures and movements do not contribute to the sensitizing of man to powerful or beneficial currents, but they are certainly not the essential. If you do not have real leanings toward the spiritual life within, no exercise will be able to fill this gap.

When I was in Japan, I spent several days in a Zen Buddhist monastery. What astonished me about the monks of this monastery and, in fact, about most of the monks I met who practise Zen, is the inexpressiveness of their faces after their meditation: no light shines from them, no life dances from their being and some of them show a great hardness in their features. Of course I am not going to pronounce on a discipline that I do not know very well, but from the point of view of true Initiatic Science, a meditation which is not a contact with the divine world, which is not capable of leaving traces of a greater love and a greater light, is not very useful.

You tell me that the aim of Za-zen is to stop thought and to create a vacuum, an emptiness. Unfortunately, I find that in certain cases, this emptiness is all too evident. You cannot take the idea of sitting and creating an emptiness as your goal in life. I do not deny that sometimes it is useful, and there are many things to be said about the practice of emptiness, but you must never forget that emptiness is there to be filled. As soon as an emptiness is felt, an element always arrives to fill it up. So if you have not purified yourself before you create this emptiness within, you will find that you attract dark and harmful entities from which you cannot defend yourself, entities which correspond to your own inner state of dilapidation and decay.

It is marvellous to become empty so that you can become an empty vessel which Heaven can fill with all its splendours, but first of all you must prepare the ground. In order to create that emptiness, call on the feminine principle in you, which is passive and receptive, but for the work of preparation you must work with your masculine principle, which is active and emissive and, by this, I mean your willpower, the ability to fight in order to protect and defend yourself. In the spiritual life it is important to be aware of the need to work with both these principles; to know when you should be receptive and when you should be emissive, when you should be projecting currents and when you should be attracting them. If people are living in disorder, if they are tense, unbalanced and ill, it is because they have not properly understood how to work with these two principles and how they should balance and adjust them.

Monstrous creatures float in the invisible world, produced by the thoughts and feelings of criminals and black magicians. These creatures look for an entry wherever they can find an open door in weak people who do not know how to protect themselves. It is only after you have purified and strengthened yourself so that you will not be invaded by dark beings that you can then safely create an emptiness within. Moreover, some symbols of Christianity, for example, the Grail, show that these practices of the void are not the sole property of oriental traditions such as Zen Buddhism. The symbol of the Grail contains a whole teaching. The cup is a feminine symbol which invites the disciple to be in a state of receptivity so that he can attract that cosmic quintessence which is the blood of Christ, the spirit of Christ. He who has received the spirit of Christ is the Holy Grail, his whole being has become a cup in which the Christ comes to dwell.

So you see, this whole question of emptiness is not clearly understood by many people. You must not rush into a spiritual practice just because it has become fashionable. Zen and many other kinds of yoga are very old disciplines brought to perfection by beings of an exceptional elevation, but they are no longer practised in the same spirit, even in the country of their own origin. I find the way in which Westerners fling themselves into these practices rather alarming. Without a precise science concerning the structure of man and his relationship with the universe, without certain rules of life that are very strict, without a high ideal of love and fraternity, it is an illusion to believe that certain positions and postures will enable you to obtain great spiritual results. It is as foolish as thinking that going to mass each Sunday, kneeling down, crossing yourself with holy water and receiving communion will mean that a Christian will receive the Holy Ghost.

Christian rituals are attracting fewer and fewer Westerners; people believe that they will reach a greater height of spirituality if they follow an Eastern teaching. Let me tell you that you can still be a great spiritualist by remaining Christian and that unfortunately you can devote yourself to all sorts of yogas and never touch the spirit.

II

Imagine that you have an orange: scientists and philosophers will tell you all sorts of things about it; its origin, its chemical make-up, its weight, its shape, its properties, the different ways of using it, its life story, its symbolism.... They know everything theoretically, but they all miss the essential, for they forget to taste it! I, who know nothing at all about these facts, eat the orange and rejoice day and night. Do the same thing yourself: be a little less learned, and eat!

But even when people want to get on the spiritual path, they do not know how to get rid of the habit, so prevalent in universities, of accumulating information, of wanting to know first this and then that, of touching on everything, being up on all that is happening, yet never doing any work on themselves. It is on account of this curiosity that mankind has made gigantic intellectual progress, but it is a very pernicious attitude for spiritual life.

In order to do real spiritual work, you must latch on to one system and delve deeply into it. If you do not, what happens to your psychic system is exactly what happens to your physical organism; if you absorb all sorts of diverse foods, you become ill and vomit. In the same way, the psychic stomach can get indigestion from all you make it swallow. What do you think it can do with a mixture of all sorts of traditions from Egypt, India, Tibet and the Andes to which you have added a dash of gnosticism, theosophy, anthroposophy and God knows what else? Do you have a mental structure solid enough to know how to direct yourself through the middle of all that? Most people do not even have a clear idea of one philosophic system, and yet they happily mix up the Kabbalah, Zen, Druids, alchemy, Catharism, Freemasonry and the Tarot!

I see that some of you are ready to accept the songs and the gestures of any tradition without realizing that by doing so, you will end up attracting all sorts of evil spirits. This is sad, because it proves that if I am not here to watch over you, you will let yourselves be swept away by anything: you will follow the first person who comes and impresses you by his magical ceremonies and fine gestures without a moment's thought of where he might be leading you. Certain practices and rites have become fashionable in the West, such as Voodoo, for example, but that does not mean that we should adopt them. I have nothing against them on their own home ground, but I do not want them here in the Universal White Brotherhood.

Nowadays, many think spirituality is responsible for unbalancing people. However, spirituality is not to be blamed if people insist on regarding it as a fair where you can find all sorts of attractions, including even the most dangerous ones of drugs, black magic and eroticism. You must understand once and for all that true spirituality is to succeed in becoming yourself the expression of the divine Teaching that you are following.

In 1938, when I began giving lectures in Paris, crowds of men and women attended who had already dabbled in goodness knows how many other Teachings. So they came to see us, and after a short time, thinking that they had learnt all there was to know, they took themselves off elsewhere to collect more information. What kind of inner work can be done under these conditions? I met some of them years later and they had continued darting hither and thither. Their ravaged faces showed that they had made no progress at all on the path of true spirituality.

I do not deny that it can be interesting and

even useful to know all the attempts people have made over the centuries to solve the mysteries of the universe and to draw nearer to the Godhead, but it is not enough. Since these religions and philosophical systems tell us only of splendour and perfection, we ourselves must make an effort to realize these ideals. Some people talk about the greatness and the wisdom of Initiates of the past when it is pitifully obvious that they themselves remain petty, weak and quite incapable of conducting their life reasonably. It is staggering! Why can they not see how ridiculous they are, how far from true spirituality!

I hope you now understand that I do not wish the Fraternity to become a market in which you can find all religions, theories and practices heaped-up in disorderly piles. It is possible that you will find ideas and methods in our Teaching which exist in other forms of spiritual paths: that is to be expected because certain fundamental truths are found everywhere. The most important thing to remember is that you must not mix the essential with the less important, and the essential will always be the necessity of working on yourself.

In the past, Initiates did not overburden their disciples with information. They revealed a few essential truths to them and then it was up to the disciples to steep themselves in these truths by

living them. The Masters put all their love, all
their soul and spirit into their words and then
the disciples received them, tasted them, digest-
ed them and lived them. It was the life behind
the words, more than the words themselves,
which nourished them. Whereas nowadays, particularly in the West, people do not have the
sensitivity which allows them to tune into the
life of these words. Instead of being nourished,
strengthened and transformed, they take notes,
coldly, instead of feeling and living something
extraordinary. All this life, which could have enlightened them, healed them and resuscitated
them, has miscarried. It passes many people by.
It is not your intellect, but your soul and your
spirit which must be in the first place and then
when that is so, you will one day be able to trav-
el through space after hearing merely a few
words.

The difference between an intellectual and a
true spiritualist is that the intellectual has chosen the horizontal plane; by wanting to extend
the sum of his information, he has developed on
the surface, whereas the spiritualist, who has
chosen the vertical plane, begins by digging and
digging... until one day oil gushes forth and he
becomes a multi-millionaire. Others, however,
live on in poverty despite all their acres of land.
If you want to work in the same way that we do,

you will find oil gushing forth and a short while from now, we will be able to give this oil freely to the whole world. Whether they like it or not, Iran and Saudia Arabia will have to agree to free oil! Interpret this how you will!

5

LEARN HOW TO BALANCE THE MATERIAL AND SPIRITUAL WORLDS

It is obvious that man is better prepared for life on the material plane than for life on the spiritual plane because the instruments which he possesses in order to live and work on the physical plane (his five senses), are much more developed than the instruments which permit him to work in the world of the spirit.

A house can be built in a few weeks whereas if you wish to create something on the spiritual plane, neither you nor anyone else can see anything. Without certainty, without clarity, you are indecisive, unhappy and so assailed with doubts that you long to give it all up and be like everybody else, throwing yourself into activities where the results are clearly visible for all to see. Of course you may do as you like, but one day, apparently in the midst of the greatest successes, you will feel that you are lacking something within. This is to be expected because you have not touched the essential, you have not planted what is necessary in the kingdom of light, wisdom and love, of power and eternity. You must understand that only your inner realizations really belong to you, because only they have their roots in you; when you leave for the other side, you will have precious stones, qualities and virtues in your soul, in your heart and in your spirit which you can take with you and thus your name will be written in the book of eternal life.

The principal advantage of the inner path lies in the value of the elements which you accumulate as they are made of the purest, most luminous material, a material which comes from God Himself. Secondly, as they truly belong to you, you are really rich. Thirdly, riches of this sort free you, so you live in peace and abundance.

The wealth of a spiritualist is something extremely subtle, even ungraspable, but if he is aware of his wealth, he is rich with all the wealth of the Lord. He possesses heaven and earth, whereas others only have a scrap of land somewhere or other.

Therefore, you see, there are two paths: one apparently brings you nothing but disappointment yet it will give you everything, so that one day you will be able to say, "I possess nothing and yet the whole universe belongs to me"; and the other path brings you all you desire but leaves you always unsatisfied because you feel that however much you cling onto your possessions, the essential has escaped you.

Everybody who truly understands the nature of their activities says about certain difficulties, "Yes, that's an occupational hazard," but it does not stop them persevering. Everybody knows that each job has its drawbacks, so why is it that spiritualists do not know the drawbacks of their calling? The fact that they lose heart and want to give up proves that they do not know the drawbacks; if they had known them in advance they would have continued with even more ardour.

The secret lies in wanting to learn something so that you can enlarge your vision. Unfortunately, however, many people when they see the immensity of a spiritual teaching are terrified and instead of rejoicing, they creep back into the safety of their shells. So much the worse for them; these people will not make great progress. If you think that you are better off with your old ideas, you are deceiving yourselves; all sorts of difficulties will come to sting, bite and harass you in order to stimulate you into evolving.

I have met so many people who say to me, "Ah Master, what an extraordinarily marvellous Teaching you give. I would love to dedicate my-

self to it, but, first of all, I have to complete a few
jobs with my husband – or my wife – or my children." All well and good, but when ten years,
twenty years later, I look at them, they still have
not managed to complete their jobs. Some have
even died without having consecrated one minute to the spiritual life. Their reasoning was
quite wrong. If you are to consecrate yourself to
the Light, to a divine Teaching, you must not
wait till everything is tidied up because nothing
is ever finally tidied up. There is always a little
detail which is imperfect. There is always a hitch
somewhere. Never expect the perfect moment;
even if nothing is sorted out, consecrate yourself
from this moment on to the spiritual life and you
will see that everything will turn out all right in
the end, without you even knowing how!

Whatever you do on the material plane is
never definitively sorted out. It is just as if you
are trying to reshape a burst rubber ball; once
you have got rid of the dent on one side, it turns
up on the other. You think you will be peaceful
once you have got your daughter married, but
then you find that she is not getting on well with
her husband, she gets divorced, and so it goes
on! The grandchildren start to arrive, the house
is too small, you have to move house... then a
child falls ill.... I tell you, it never ends! Do not
keep planning to consecrate yourself to the spiri-

tual life one day in the future, but realize it is precisely because of the spiritual life that you will find the best solutions to all your current problems.

It goes without saying that you must keep everything in proportion. Yesterday a brother said to me, "Master, I have decided to organize my life so that from now on, I will no longer have to spend my time and energy in the world." I congratulated him, but I also advised him not to exaggerate too much in the other direction, by behaving as if the world and society do not exist. I do not recommend people to become anti-social parasites! You must learn how to balance life in both the outer and inner worlds. I had to face this problem when I was young and you, too, will have to resolve the question of how to live in the world and have relations with it whilst at the same time keeping in first place the life of the soul and spirit, for this life is the essential.

According to the way you balance these two aspects of the material and the spiritual, you show how intelligent you are and how great your love and willpower are. Nothing is more difficult to achieve than this balance; some people find that their temptation is to bury themselves in materialism, forgetting the life of the spirit, whilst others concern themselves only with their spiritual life and forget their material existence.

There is a third solution but each person has to
find it for himself, as each case is different. Fun-
damentally, of course, all people possess the
same nature, the same quintessence, the same
needs; they have all come from the hands of the
Creator, from the same workshops, if you like,
but their degree of evolution is not the same.
Add to this that their temperaments and voca-
tions in this life are different and you will see
that each person has to solve this problem for
himself and not think the answer lies in copying
his neighbour. Those who feel compelled to
have a family will not see the solution in the
same terms as those who prefer to stay celibate.
The person who needs a lot of activity will not
be able to lead the same life as someone with a
meditative, contemplative temperament.

Everybody has his own path, his mission,
and even if you take your Master as a model,
you must always develop in the way that suits
your own nature. You have to sing the part
which has been given to you, aware of the notes,
the beat and the rhythm; you have to sing it
with your voice which is certainly not that of
your Master, but that is not important. The one
really important thing is to sing your part perfectly, conforming to the only absolutely true
philosophy, the eternal philosophy of the Initiates.

6

A MASTER IS A MIRROR
REFLECTING THE TRUTH

I

If a man does not know himself, if he is not aware of his gifts and his weaknesses, of his potential and his deficiencies, he will not achieve much in life nor have harmonious relationships with others. This lack of knowledge leads directly to all sorts of complications, collisions, confusions and misfortunes. We need to know who we are, what we represent, what we are capable of doing or not doing.... Yet people make constant mistakes over how to evaluate themselves, which lead to very serious consequences. Everything, from business partnerships to marriage, risks failure if there is not a fundamental and clear knowledge of yourself and of others. True wisdom begins by knowing yourself.

How is this wisdom achieved? Man is provided with the necessary organs for knowledge, yet he is made in such a way that he cannot see himself. He can see the outer world and others in it, but he cannot see himself. If you want to

see yourself in the physical world, you have to
have an object such as a mirror (or the surface of
water) which reflects you back to yourself. You
can only see yourself both physically and psy-
chologically through something external to
yourself; you need other people to discover who
you are. However, as they are never completely
clear and unselfish, they cannot be an impeccable mirror and so they reflect back a distorted
image. For reasons they are rarely aware of, people have sympathies and antipathies which lead
them to exaggerate the qualities and faults of
others. Enemies amplify each others' faults to
the point where they cannot acknowledge the
slightest good trait in the other.

You may feel that if that is the way things
are, the way to learn about yourselves must be
by reading books. However, everything depends
on the kind of books you choose and at what level they will help you. Your next suggestion may
be that life will teach you to know yourself. Now
you are making sense! That is undoubtedly true,
but unfortunately life takes a long time over its
lessons and they will be very costly for you, too.
You will indeed know yourself a bit better, but
the damage will be irreparable. The most effec-
tive, most wise and most economic way I advise
you to use is to ask Heaven to place you in front
of a perfect mirror. By this I mean that you

should find a being of great self-denial, of great disinterestedness, who has nothing to gain by deceiving you: in other words, a true Master. Find an Initiate and ask him, "Who am I? What is there in me? What weaknesses do I have to combat, what wealth and talents must I develop? What work have I been predestined to do?" And he, in his disinterestedness, will communicate with Heaven and give you impeccable replies.

If this mirror begins to reflect some of your faults, should you become angry with it? On the contrary, you should thank Heaven that you are able to avoid great catastrophes and that you will spare yourself and others great unhappiness. However, people do not like to see what they are really like; they prefer to live in their illusions. A Master knows in advance what will happen when he opens his mouth. People are not going to say, "Yes, of course, you are absolutely right," but will protest, "No, no, you have made a mistake, it is not like that at all, by any stretch of the imagination!" Evidently the Master can be mistaken, but never them!

It is difficult for Initiates to know how to make people accept the truth. For example, a sister comes to see me and says, "Master, I want you to tell me what my weaknesses and faults are so that I can correct them." "You won't be angry at what I say?" "No, no, not at all. I will

accept everything." I just start to say a few words
and immediately she begins to cry. So I say, "If
you weep, I shall have to stop, because you are
so overwrought by your distress that you listen
to none of my explanations, you cannot even
hear them. If you want to understand something,
you must calm your emotions. How can you expect to understand anything when you have
started to be pained and distressed right at the
start?"

Do not imagine that this is only true for
those whom I receive personally. When I am
talking in the Great Hall, I see that some of you
are unhappy with my explanations and that, instead of listening to me, you shut yourselves off
in disapproval. It is useless coming to the Bonfin
if you are going to hear and understand nothing.
You must come with the one goal of learning
truths which you do not yet know and which
will help you transform your life. If you are to
do that, you must accept being a little shaken-
up. If I were to commiserate with you, always
saying, "Poor old chap, how miserable it is for
you!" what good would that do? When a child
falls and hurts himself, he cries a little, but if to
cheer him up you say, "Oh you poor dear, it's
terrible, how badly you have been hurt!" he will
cry ten times harder and twice as long! Whereas
if you say, "Up you hop, it was only a little

bump," he jumps up and within two minutes, his tears have dried and the whole thing is over and done with. Do not think that you should always be sympathetic, because that is often the best way to increase people's weakness and laziness.

A Master's task is not merely to manifest much love and tenderness. He must also be severe on his disciples by telling them certain truths for their progress and advancement. It is hard luck if what he says does not please the disciples! If I worried about your reactions and your opinions of me, I would get nothing done at all. Some of you have told me that when I showed you your weaknesses, you detested me. It does not affect me at all if I am detested, because I have a good thick skin, but if I am to help you, I am obliged to shake you up. Those who go on thinking that they are impeccable whereas in reality they behave in a way that is very ordinary, if not downright bad, cannot ever make any real progress. It is much better to learn certain truths even if they cause suffering at first; these uncomfortable moments will soon pass, but the light of truth will lead to a change in behaviour and so to progress. One fine day you will see that I was so useful that you will search for me on the furthest planets in order to thank me!

When you are ill, you think it makes perfect sense to swallow disagreeable remedies to make you better. You have to do the same thing in the spiritual realm; you have been ill for a long time and you need treatment. There will be no hope of improvement if you do not accept the remedy.

If I were to allow you to continue as you are, without saying a word, Heaven would be angry with me, and would ask, "Are you a coward? Do you fear to tell the truth in case it distresses someone? Is everything to go wrong through your fault?" Personally, I would love to make you happy, but my work and my responsibilities have also to be considered. Moreover, a Master who shuts his eyes is not useful. You see, disciples have no idea what they should expect from their Master. What is the use of a Teacher if he allows you to make mistakes without enlightening and correcting you? I myself would never follow such a Master!

I know what I am doing and I realize the situation very clearly. I know that if I am to win your friendship, I must deceive you and compliment you, "Ah! You are unique! I have travelled all over the world and I have never met anyone so wise and intelligent." If I looked in the dictionary for the rarest, most poetic words to say to you, then I could be sure that you would adore me. However, I am no fool; I know what is useful and what is not, therefore I know what I lose by being sincere with you. I have accepted to be the loser in order that you should gain the benefit.

Why is it that people always want to be complimented? People have this weakness of self-deception for they could not bear to live without it. What would become of humanity if people did not employ deception? Tell a decrepit old woman the truth, that she is a real sight, and she will never forgive you. Tell her that she is a sight for sore eyes, that she is still young, pretty and lovely and see how she smiles and laughs and wriggles with pleasure! Indeed, if she is rich, she will give you her fortune, and all because you have told her a lie. You must understand I am only stating what I have seen and that I am not advising you to act in this way!

Most people will not tell you the truth about your faults and weaknesses, because they are afraid of losing your services or gaining your enmity. Behind their apparently caring, sensitive attitude, therefore, they have a personal motive, and so they leave you with your faults which grow bigger over the years. A true Initiate, however, behaves quite differently. He has no personal motive, no fear, and nothing to lose; because he knows the truth he has gained everything. He will not hesitate, therefore, to show you your weaknesses, all the things which hold you down in hellish regions and hinder you from going to the land of light, to Paradise. He dares tell you all the things you do which make you ill and unhappy, and he wants to give you all the methods which can remedy your imperfections and your deficiencies.

The Master is, of course, extremely careful how he tells the truth to his disciple. At the beginning, the disciple is like a child who needs his mother to nurse him, protect him and caress him. After a certain time, the mother has to wean the growing child from the breast and in the same way the Master has to wean his disciple. It is not cruelty or indifference; the time has come when the child can learn to feed itself. In the same way animals are very tender with their little ones, but after a while the mothers reject their offspring, giving them a few cuffs with their paws to say, "Off you go, get on by yourselves now, you no longer need me."

An Initiate considers all his pupils, his disciples, as children who first of all need gentleness and encouragement and then, as they grow up, and are steadier on their legs, he gives them a few blows, by telling them the truth. However, he does not chase them away; he keeps them near him and he begins to shape them, to sculpt and model them or (to use another metaphor) he gives them a course of treatment with the truth, including several injections and a few operations. Some people find truth very difficult both to hear and to bear, but for the disciple who has decided to evolve and advance, it is magnificent; he will even beg his Master to tell him the truth, because he can see that certain things are fettering him as a prisoner, and causing him to do stupid things.

Only those who are truly touched by the grace of God ask for the truth, however painful it may be. Often when I have wanted to draw the attention of certain brothers and sisters to some of their very marked faults, they begin to reply, "Oh no, it is not true, I am not at all like that!" If I speak to them about their qualities, they approve and are amazed by my perceptiveness and the truth of my remarks, yet when I speak of their faults, it is quite clear I have made a mistake!

So this is the method of true Initiates; when it is necessary, they will speak the truth without fearing the loss of their friends. If the friends are irritated, wounded and embittered by these utterly truthful remarks... well, if they are not honest and sincere enough to recognize the truth, then it is better to lose them. Is there any point in an Initiate being surrounded by people who are so dishonest with themselves?

An Initiate is not afraid of losing his disciples; he knows that a true disciple will not leave him. The disciple will think it all out correctly, saying, "I trust my Master, he has nothing to gain from wounding or crushing me, or from my death. If he speaks to me in this way, he must have his reasons. As he knows better than I how I should act, I will trust him and accept that what he is saying is for my good." At that moment, the Master, who is watching him, will rejoice to see that there he has a real disciple who is worthy of initiation. Nothing can surpass receiving initiation and wisdom, knowing the truth and being in the light. However, you must first have conquered this lower nature in yourself, a nature which is always irritated, wounded, outraged or vengeful.

Have you any idea of the number of people whom the truth has irritated and who then sought revenge on me? They are more numerous than the hairs on your head! Did I rob them, cheat them, crush them or murder them? On the contrary I gave them a love which they had never found even in their own families. However, I dared to tell them the truth and so that was the end of it all. They did not realize that if they did not correct certain weaknesses, they would be held back, shackled, with the road of their evolution blocked. In the spiritual world, there are barriers that cannot be crossed unless certain conditions have been fulfilled. When you want to have the laws and the beauties of higher regions revealed to you, when you want to meet the luminous beings and see their colours, their music, their perfume and all the order, symmetry and splendour of these regions, you will not be accepted unless the inhabitants find that you are worthy. To be worthy you must at least accept that you have faults and do something about correcting them.

Your weak point, which hinders you from getting through to real Initiation is that you are often too easily offended. Does your teacher dare to reprove you? Has he dared to point out some of your weaknesses? He ought never to do so; he ought to behave like a well-brought-up person, never mentioning any of your deficiencies, and never trying to improve you. If he continues, you will leave him and that will be a real punishment for him.... So you see, people say that they love the truth, that they are searching for it, but this attitude of theirs does not show great love of the truth.

Many of you have said to me, "Master, if you had any idea of the state I was in when you told me that!... But afterwards I saw, I understood and I was so happy! I thank you from the bottom of my heart." Why not be happy straightaway? Why do you have to go through horrendous states first? It is such a pity. It is so much better to be happy immediately, to be grateful and to understand. My motive is never to demolish someone but to help him change, to become beautiful and be saved. You must realize that it is not the fact that matters but the motive. You can be given a gift with criminal intentions; with your lack of enlightenment, you see only the present and so you rejoice, yet afterwards you die of poisoning. People often make such mistakes. You must not go by appearances, but by the goal. As for me, the goal of all I do is that it should help you, and if you are sincere, you cannot but recognize this.

I know perfectly well that each time I shake somebody up, I am running enormous risks.... If he works for the radio, he will broadcast a talk against me.... If he is a journalist, he will write an article criticizing me.... If he is a painter, he will caricature me. I know all this, but I accept it all in order to help him see things more clearly. I am not concerned with what happens to me: he may become my enemy, and that is unfortunate; but I am doing this for his own good. Many years later, events will show that I was right; he will remember and will understand that I wanted what was best for him, that I wanted him to be free, rich and loved by all.

I have often told you that I see myself as a dentist. I know my trade. I do not have modern equipment, my pliers are old-fashioned. I make no use of anaesthetic so, of course, when I pull teeth, people shout. However, when it has all healed over and everything has got better, the patient is happy. Recently a sister came to me and said, "Master, would you please give me another good shaking up as you did the other day?" I asked her why she wanted it and she replied, "Because it did me so much good!" I looked at her and saw she was sincere. I said, "Ah no, things do not happen like that. I only stir someone up when I feel that it is the right moment, and today I am not going to do it, as it is not the right moment," and so she went away, empty-handed. People think that I act upon a whim, whereas everything I do is determined, weighed and precisely calculated to gain a particular result. There is no point in treating someone badly; what do you gain by that? What is valuable is to heal someone, to do him good, to make him think and look at himself once again. It is clear that the brothers and sisters do not know me yet, they do not understand the reasons for my behaviour and so think that I do

what I feel like doing without taking the timing
into account.

From now on, have a bit more confidence in
my methods. I have still got many more which
you do not yet know. When I shake you up,
when I do an "operation," I apply a method
which you do not know, but it is always for your
own good, to take something away from you
which has made you suffer and which hinders
your evolution. So now, if you have no confidence in me, do what you want, you are perfectly free. I must however tell you in advance that
you will have no results, no advantages, but only
devastation and debts to deal with. Whereas
with my methods, you will end as kings and
lords, always rich and victorious. So then it is up
to you to choose.

Understand from now on that I dare to be-
rate you often because I am unbiased. If I had a
personal interest in it, I would not dare as I
would be afraid of losing you and fear is a very
bad adviser. My daring, my "cheek," shows how
unbiased I am. As you do not know how to dis-
cern what this behaviour corresponds to within
me, you think that it is bad temper, or a bad
mood or a lack of upbringing... that I need lick-
ing into shape. No, not at all. You have never
seen that this audacity comes from my lack of
bias. Become unbiased yourselves and you will

see the same thing; you will tell people the truth without fearing that they might leave you, since you do not wish to gain anything from them.

A teacher tells the truth to his disciple in order to help him. If the disciple does not understand this and does not want to be helped, he is perfectly free to leave and others will come in his place one day who are really searching for the truth. What can a Master do with people who are so easily offended? Great princes and mighty scholars cannot bear that anyone should make the slightest comment about them, even if it is for their own good!

For the sake of argument, let us suppose that I have committed an injustice towards you by criticizing you. If you have understood what I have said to you today, you would not dwell on what I said, but on the contrary, you would go on behaving impeccably. When you came to see me again, my eyes would widen with surprise, "My goodness, how marvellous!" You would have won a victory, I would take back what I said and bow down before you!

You have the right to work on yourself, to become better and to win the victory, but you have no right to be irritated. Are you irritated? Your reactions are totally unimportant and I do not give tuppence for those who get irritated instead of getting on with the work. I have shaken

them up precisely so that they will roll up their
sleeves and set to work yet, there they are, sulking away.... It is far easier to sulk than to resolve
your problems, by learning how to put a bit
more love and a bit more light into your life. So
now, get on with the work so that you can come
and say to me, "Look, dear Master, you were
wrong." I will be able to answer, "It is true, I
made a mistake." I have never said it up till now
because you have not given me the chance; you
stay sulking.

So then, what are you waiting for? It is time
to get moving, to do everything to convince me
of my blindness and my mistakes. Prove it to me
and I will be very happy. If I have judged you in-
accurately, you have the right to show me that
you are more noble, more generous than I think.
However, if you do not show me, I am forced to
acknowledge that it was I who was right. It does
not do me any good to be right, in fact I am unhappy when I am right. I would prefer to be
wrong, I would prefer to be mistaken. For example, if I say that someone has no love or discernment, and then he shows by his attitude that he
is full of love or is magnificently discerning, it is
a wonderful surprise for me! Yes, you see in certain cases, I am very happy to acknowledge that
I was mistaken.

II

You are very far from understanding the value of the truths that a Master brings you. Other things are so much more important for you and even though they are more than likely to make you unhappy and ill, you do not care as you find them so much more important, more attractive, more appetizing. You are, of course, absolutely free in your choice, but without this light I bring you, wait and see what a state you will find yourself in eventually!

Perhaps you think I exaggerate my importance. You are free to think whatever you like. It makes no difference at all to me whether I am appreciated or not. If I talk to you in the way I do, it is so that you will no longer have to spend your time running to and fro but will be able at last to build your future on solid foundations. Otherwise you will always be busy, running after tiny glittering things that catch your attention and which, when you have got them, will only bring you unhappiness, as you have not got the inner light to let you see that, in fact, they were harmful. Why do you have this lack of discernment? It is because you have not got sufficient awareness of the value of your Teacher.

Realize, in any case, that I am not greedy for power; all I think about is controlling myself. What happiness could I find in the enslavement of others? I find happiness elsewhere. Some of you have asked me to be like those gurus who impose themselves on others and expect their disciples to prostrate themselves before them. You think that is a weakness on my part that I do not wish to behave like this. What a peculiar idea! In fact, if anything always shocked me in India, it was seeing how certain Masters allowed their disciples to prostrate themselves before them. I have even said to them, "What pleasure do you get from seeing these poor people at your feet? Who are you, that they should throw themselves on the ground? I would never accept this from my disciples...." This is absolutely true; some people have wanted to prostrate themselves before me, but I have made them get up immediately. These gurus never said anything to my reproaches, but I understood what they were thinking: they had prostrated themselves before their Masters and so it was perfectly normal for their disciples to do it to them.

However, I do not want to concern myself with that : these habits come from a centuries' old tradition and it is difficult to make Indians understand how shocking they are for Westerners.

Even if he possesses all powers, a Master must stay simple and the fact that I am making you become aware of the value of a Teacher is not going to change my attitude to you. I love treating all the brothers and sisters with respect and love. Even if I say a few words to you on the value of my work to you, it is not going to change me. Perhaps you will change, and that is desirable, because the more you appreciate what I say and put it into practise, the more you will progress. In any case, whatever you do, I will go on with my work. Of course, I will profit if you advance because I shall have more friends, but you will gain the most, because you will be planting seeds which will one day give fruits for you to gather.

Therefore, from now on, do not regard it as a weakness if I do not behave like certain Indian masters and do not try to impose my will on yours. If you could see the way I deal with myself, you would see how I give orders and impose my will, but I never do it with you. What goes on within me is quite different, but why should I give you orders? You are children of God and if anyone should give you orders, it is God Himself. You say, "Yes, but sometimes you shake us up and fly into a passion...." That is true, I am sometimes obliged to insist on particular points, on certain values, but I never compel you to act in any predetermined way.

In my youth, I was most impressed by the fact that my mother never forced me to do anything. She would always say, "Now then, if you do this, you will have this result and if you do that, you will have that result." She always showed me both paths and their consequences. I do the same; I sometimes shake someone up and say terrible things which he needs to hear, but I never force anyone to do anything.

However, even if I do not succeed in convincing people, I do not get despondent; I stay calm, because I have a powerful collaborator in my work which is life itself. I may only be an inadequate teacher, but life is perfect at the job. You can cry as much as you like, tear your hair out in despair, and it will have no effect. Life is implacable; no weeping or gnashing of teeth will move it to compassion. When you have an accident, when you are ruined, when your friends, your wife, your children leave you, when you have lost your job or your house has burnt down, then you really have something to think about. Unfortunately, it does not automatically lead you to finding the truth; you may weep and wish you were dead, but you rarely understand anything.

Life corrects man, shakes him up and nearly kills him, but it gives no explanations. For explanations you must go to a Master, and so between life and a Master, the poor wretch learns a thing or two. Just as some garages, or better still, doctors, refer their clients to other specialists, I refer my clients to Life. When I see that I have not managed to enlighten someone and make him wise, I turn to my associate Life and say, "Listen, will you have a go at this one because he is a very tough nut." "Right!" says Life. Then when my client has been battered about a bit and badly treated without understanding why, Life refers him back to me so that I can explain it all to him. So you see how Life and I play ball together! My goodness, yes, the two of us are well organized! If you do not pay attention to what I am saying to you each day, I will let Life have a go at you. I am all sweetness and Light, but Life is terrible and will batter you despite all your cries until you are nearly destroyed and then it will toss you back to me. It has already happened to many people and can take two, ten, twenty years or very much longer.

Many brothers and sisters who wanted to distance themselves from the truths of the Teaching, because they needed the wisdom of experience, have come back twenty years later, broken and without their fine feathers. They do not know why all these horrors have happened to them and yet it is so simple; they have an inferior tendency which they have fed and nourished, thinking that by giving it all it wants they would be happy. This tendency is magnetically linked to certain substances, entities and realities of a determined nature in the cosmos and so it can only bring them unhappiness and disasters. So, in fact, it is they themselves who have attracted all these unhappy events.

Life on earth is a school and so what you find in school is lessons, lessons on all sides. Until you have understood that, you will be harassed by destiny. The invisible world sends Masters to help people's evolution and if these Masters are not accepted then other teachers such as illnesses, misery, difficulties will come and these teachers are implacable. If you do not wish to undergo their terrible lessons, accept me. It is so much wiser. If you do not wish to accept the divine laws of your own accord you will have to learn them with the aid of a few blows from the teacher's cane.

It would be very easy for me to decide that I will never concern myself with your problems or point out to you certain things in your way of thinking and acting which slow down your evolution. If I withdraw, you will overload yourself more and more, tying yourself in such knots that you will be crushed under your burdens and entangled in inextricable situations. Would that be helpful to you?

Some of you will remember that when I have drawn your attention to what was defective, I also helped in solving the problem. When you know who the enemy is which lurks beneath a fault, a bad habit, a misconception, then you are able to battle against it. However, if you do not know on which side you are being attacked, you are powerless. Nothing is worse than ignorance of the origin of your difficulties, sufferings and unhappiness, because in this case you keep firing your cartridges wildly into space until you have used up all your ammunition and yet you have won no victory. At least when you know where your enemy is and how he behaves, you have the means to defend yourself and sooner or later, you will succeed in toppling him.

One day you will understand me and will say, "My God, blessed be the day when I met the Master. He gave us all the methods we need to surmount our difficulties, he was our best friend, but we did not understand it until too late." Yes, I emphasize this, I underline it, in the hope that one day you will understand the exceptional chance that has been given to you to

resolve all your problems and help you progress
on your path of evolution. You are thinking,
"My goodness, what pride, what vanity!"
Think what you like, it makes no difference to
me, but take what I say seriously and set to
work!

7

A MASTER IS THERE ONLY TO GIVE LIGHT

I

It is very difficult to do good. All my life I have asked myself, "What is the best way to help people?" I saw that if one day they were given food, the next day they were hungry again, because the stomach is a bottomless pit which demands food each day.... If they were given clothes, these get old and tattered after a while and have to be replaced. If you give them a house, they are going to need money one day or another to repair it. If you give them money, it will soon get spent.... If you have had any dealings with people, you find that they are never satisfied. If you give them a house, they wonder why you have not given them a palace, and if you give them millions of pounds they are angry that it is not billions. It is therefore impossible to help people in this way; either the help is not definitive or people are unhappy because they are always expecting more. So how can one help them?

Think, for example, of a man who has a heavy burden to carry. It is so heavy that he can hardly lift it up. There you are, strong and hearty; you take the burden on your shoulders and all is well. Yes, but the following day this man is going to have other burdens to carry and as you cannot always be with him, what is he going to do? Imagine then, that you have a secret which will allow him not only to carry the burdens without getting crushed by them but even to carry them happily; you pass this secret on to him and then for the rest of his life he can manage his burdens all by himself. Is it not the best way to help people: to show them a way to help themselves? Of course it is better, much, much better. The light of Initiatic Science is this way because in all circumstances, this science can provide the solutions.

That is why all my life I have worked unceasingly to find this light because I know that when I have given it to you, you will be able to deal with all difficulties by yourself, without me. Without light, not only will the good you do be fleeting, but people will not even be grateful. What they must be given is a spiritual element which will be engraved within. So many people are unaware of this. When they want to do good, instead of thinking about giving this spiritual element that can never be erased, they give something material. Instead of giving the essential, they give little scraps, in the form of jewels or cars, thinking that these are what make other people happy. You must learn to give the essential element.

Should you think that I have no idea of all your difficulties, you are mistaken. I know them because, I, too, have been through them. I have lived them and it is enough for me to look at someone to understand the difficulties that he has been through, because they are written on his face. If you wonder why I have not helped him, why I have no compassion, well, here again I have to give you explanations.

Had I all the powers imaginable, Heaven would not allow me to take your difficulties away from you. It is up to you to make the effort; to learn, to stretch your muscles, because that will be useful for eternity. If you expect someone to do it all for you, to take away your suffering, illness and misery, it can be done; there are people who are capable of doing that, but a really wise person would never do it because he knows that not only will it not help you, it will hinder you. He will therefore give you methods and knowledge but will expect it to be you who applies them because when you do, it will be you that grows, you who will become stronger, and that is true evolution.

Unfortunately, people are only used to counting on material help, on external things such as machines or medicine, rather than using the possibilities the Creator has put inside them. When they meet a Master, they have exactly the same attitude: instead of learning to develop their spiritual faculties with his help, they expect the Master to do everything for them; the Master has to teach them, purify them, heal them, find solutions to all their problems and make them happy and rich. Yes, this attitude of expecting everything from the outside is so widespread that even spiritualists have adopted it. A Master for them is a fellow who will come to their rescue, save them and, moreover, carry all their burdens. They see him as a useful sort of donkey! Analyse yourself and see if I am not right.

Many who come to this Teaching expect everything from me: that I will make them healthy, wealthy and find them marriage partners; if I do not do it, they are disappointed and leave me. There really are people whom I have never met who write asking me to find them a wife or a husband. How can I make them understand that that is not what I am concerned with at all? It is a very delicate area and those who get involved have to be aware of their responsibilities. The task of a Master is not that of marrying and divorcing people. Of course, in certain cases, when young brothers and sisters that I know come to ask me my advice, I give it... yet even then I do not always do so, because the situation is so delicate.

What a curious mentality people have! They expect me to do everything for them, right down to choosing their partners. When they have children, they expect me to invite angels and archangels to come and incarnate in their home. Oh no, that is not my job, not at all. The one thing that they can expect from me is bumps and jolts to shake them into learning how to do things for themselves. Even if I had the power to grant all their requests, I would not do it, because this is not the way to help them. In fact, even if I had the power to heal all illnesses, not only would I not do so, but I would even add others! Does that outrage you? I would add more, but at the same time I would give the methods whereby they could overcome all illnesses. If I were to cure their illnesses, they would still go on living stupidly and excessively and so they would become ill again. When I had gone, they would then remain ill for all eternity. So you see, healing people is no real solution. Therefore I tell you that my way of dealing with it is to add more burdens to your back so that you will learn to become stronger and more resistant.

A true disciple must not expect that life will be easy for him or for his nearest and dearest. Most fathers and mothers want their children to have smoothly flowing lives, with lots of success and money; of course they want this because they love their children, but it is a childish love which has not understood how their children really should evolve. Of course I am not saying that parents should long for their children to suffer – not at all – they should not even think of it. Their desire should only be that their children become benefactors of humanity and it is up to Heaven to decide what experiences their children must pass through in order to become just that. Heaven may send them illnesses, enemies and disgrace, but that does not matter. They will go so far, so incredibly far, that there will not remain one trace of all these difficulties, not even a memory. Parents love their children, but what will become of them if all difficulties are cleared out of their paths? They will just grow up stupid.

Understand quite clearly that I am not here to bother about your illnesses, your problems and your divorces. If you are having to go through these things, there is probably a karmic reason for it. The only thing I am here for is to help you help yourselves to real freedom, so that you stay strong despite all the difficulties on your path. I am not here to heal you, to cheer you up, to resolve all your problems (besides, I have not got the time, it would take me all eternity to deal with your problems and what problems they are!) but my job is to stimulate you, to show you the highest ideal. If you long to reach the highest ideal, you will be able to solve everyone of your problems. Whereas if I overcome all your difficulties for you, you will always stay weak, puny, vulnerable and then what will you do when I am not with you anymore?

Yesterday, on television, there was a programme showing that more and more people are going to clairvoyants, mediums and magicians in order to solve all their money problems, their health problems and also so that they can be exorcised and have spells removed. It is quite extraordinary, they do nothing themselves in order to conquer these difficulties, in order to see more clearly and to get stronger, but expect somebody else to do it for them. Even supposing that someone is capable of unbewitching them, they are so weak that someone else will be able to put a spell on them once again. Everybody expects that someone else will heal, comfort and encourage them, and it is for this reason they continue ignorant, puny and vulnerable.

Ah well, here it is not like that; here nobody cheers you up, nobody comforts you and makes you better, but you are given weapons, tools, methods whereby you may become intelligent, powerful and invincible, and that is infinitely more useful. Look for the easy way and there will be nobody and nothing to help you. Here lies your mistake, because if anybody really can help you, not just for two or three days, but for eternity, it is certainly me. However, you only want one thing, to stand there with your mouth open ready to swallow any pill and it does not matter to you whether or not it is a mere place-bo. When will you understand that you have got to learn to do all the work yourselves?

Here you are given all the methods, so at least try to make use of them! Even if the great Masters performed prodigious miracles to heal and protect you, how long do you think it would last? It all depends on you; if you know how to make use of the light and of the keys which you are given here, then the change would be defini-tive, because you yourself, your soul and spirit, have joined in the work.

I know human nature. You would love to hear me say, "Come unto me and I will save you from all dangers, I will heal all your illnesses and I will make you happy." No, no, no, dear brothers and sisters, I will not say it to you, be-cause it is not true. If anyone does say it to you, know that he wants to deceive you. What I say is, "Count on the great truths which I give you, accept them, feed them, give them life, make them strong within you, then you will see the results."

Today I may, perhaps, have destroyed some of your illusions, but I did it in the interests of truth and for your own good.

II

You always rely on me. That is all very well, except you must realize that even the greatest Master can do nothing unless the disciple possesses at least the seed of certain virtues which the Master can nourish and help bear fruit.

If parents want to have a child who will be successful later on in some particular sphere, they have to think about planting the appropriate elements in him right from the moment of conception, because no teacher can develop qualities in a child if there is not at least the seed there. So do not accuse a Master of being incapable of making you divine, if you do not have divine elements within. If, however, you do possess them, he is more capable than anyone else of making them bear fruit. In the same way, alchemists say that you cannot make gold if there is not at least one particle of gold at the beginning.

It is indeed true that a Master can do many things, but only for those who already have divine aspirations, who have a high ideal, otherwise he can do nothing. That is why a Master never tries to force anyone into a particular direction because he knows the pointlessness of such an action. If someone is closed and uncomprehending, a Master will leave him in peace. This is yet another of the differences between a true and a false Master. A false Master will do everything he can to make you take the direction he wants. A true Master, who knows that he has no right to compel people, will talk to you, will give you explanations, will pray for you, but that is all he will do. If you want to choose hell, he will explain what is awaiting you, but he will not stop you. Those who want to destroy themselves are allowed to, nobody has the right to hinder them, not even God Himself. If you want proof, look at the way He lets people do whatever stupid things they want, falling flat on their faces.... He respects their freedom of choice.

You could say, "You never leave us free, you harangue us in your conferences and keep on hammering home your points." Yes, that is true, but all the same there is something you have to admit, which is that though I talk and explain, I never force you to do anything. I try to influence you, it is true; think of the sun, it tries to influence you, too. It shines and warms and that is an influence. If you do not want to be affected, it is up to you to go and hide yourself. Stars, mountains, lakes, rivers, plants, animals and people are all able to influence you, but you have complete freedom to go away or to stay under their influence. Does a pretty girl not influence and affect all the boys? Yes, but you cannot criticize her for it, because that is how things happen. Those who do not want to be affected by her, should not go and dance with her!

So then I agree that I influence you. Why should I be an exception to this rule? However, I do not force you. If you have come to hear me, that means that you are willing to be influenced. I did not come to find you, you came here of your own free will. Freedom means being able to choose whether you put yourself under certain influences. From the moment you agree to put yourself under the influence of my voice, my looks, my gestures, my thoughts, you can lay no blame on me. If you do not want to be under my influence, do not come. Even so, I cannot suppress everything in me under the pretext of leaving you your liberty. The only thing I have no right to do is to influence you towards evil, by which I mean to push you towards despair, doubt, revolt or hatred. I have, however, the right to enlighten you, to give you peace and to lead you towards God and that is what I have always tried to do. You should even pray that I carry on for as long as possible, because it is you who will benefit. However, if you do not want it, that is your affair.

I have warned so many people about what awaits them if they continue on their present path. I do not let people wander off without enlightening them, but they choose not to believe me: they know, better than I do, what they ought to be doing. Of course, when they come across the difficulties that I foresaw – and they were so easy to foresee – I am the one who has to put everything together again, and if I do not do it, then once again they blame me. So, quite clearly, what I should do is not to teach people and help them along the good road, but allow them to do all their stupid things in peace and then my job is to put right everything which they have destroyed! Supposing that I were to do that, do you think that it would really be the solution? No, it would be worse. As long as people have not suffered, or understood anything, it would be much worse. You must let people suffer a little until they begin to realize that they must become a little wiser and develop some discernment. If you smooth out all their difficulties, they will never really understand their situation.

They will never really appreciate the value of things, but will always stay unaware and ungrateful.

Many parents have not understood this. With the excuse that they love their children, they never let them suffer or burn themselves a little in order to learn a lesson. At the slightest problem, they rush in to organize everything. That is not true love, nor is it the way God and Nature act. You must help people, by giving them explanations, by enlightening them and then, when they have begun to be aware of the situation and to suffer, you can do something about lightening their burdens. It is at that moment that they will appreciate the help you give and then they will become wise and sensible; they will make good resolutions. If you do not act in this way, not only will you do no good to anybody, but you will encourage folly, crime and all sorts of transgressions.

Here you are given the essential, so why not start working with these elements? These great truths are not to be taken lightly, but should be absorbed profoundly into your life, because perhaps you may no longer have anyone to help you. You must realize that you have no right to do whatever you fancy, you must always ask, "Is what I want to do the will of Heaven or just my own desire?" People lack discernment and even when they know what they ought to do, they do just the opposite.

A person comes to me and says, "Master, tell me how to act so that I can get out of my difficulties and I will do what you advise." Fine, I want to help him, I tell him what to do and he promises to do it, but two minutes later, he has forgotten all my advice and is carrying on in the same old way. Why? Because there are other tendencies in man, other beings which advise him and lead him to his ruin and these are the entities he listens to. What must he do in order not to be led astray? He must hang on like a limpet and not listen to any of them. Since he wanted to listen to his Master, why not listen? He does quite the opposite. Should his Master then ask him, "Why have you not done what you promised?" he will weep unhappily and deeply regret his behaviour. He is aware, and yet still he falls into this position through leaving himself open to evil spirits.

If you have done everything possible to lose control over yourself, letting yourself be invaded by inferior beings who are only out to trip you up, you can accuse nobody but yourself. What you must then do is to say, "I have not worked in the right way, I have not studied as I should, so I will take myself in hand and put things right." Obviously this will take time, because you have spent years twisting your mind with all sorts of chaotic thoughts and activities and you cannot put it all right in a few minutes. You will have to work in the right way for many years, in order to obtain good results.

People do not know the laws; they have spent their lives doing stupid things and when they decide to change direction they think that they can repair all the damage that their folly has caused in two minutes. They are free to dream what they want, but unfortunately the hard facts are that it is impossible. It took a long time to destroy yourself, so it is going to take a long time to rebuild yourself. People have the most amazing naïvety. They really think that it is possible in one fell swoop to put everything right which they have damaged. If a Master is not capable of transforming a debauchee or a criminal into a saint in one day, that proves that he is no Master! What amazing reasoning!

Over the years I have given you many ways of purifying and protecting yourself with the light and with colours so that you become able to form an impenetrable barrier around yourself against evil spirits. Light is able to distance and destroy these spirits by its intense vibrations. That is why you must really work with the light and, by meditation and prayer, make this light come into you. In reality, when I say light, I mean beneficent beings, and once these are installed in you they will prevent bad influences from entering.

This does not mean that once you have a powerful aura, a fortress of light, you will never be disturbed or attacked. Unfortunately, so long as one is on earth, one is never safe from assaults and conflicts. However, when one is well-defended and barricaded by the light, it is quite different. Even the strongest, the most powerful of Initiates, have to keep thinking of erecting a barrier of light, circles of flames between them and the spirits of evil who come and attack them, yet ignorant and weak people think that they have no need for protection. It is time for you to understand the importance, the seriousness of all that I am saying to you, otherwise you will be at the mercy of all harmful currents.

The ignorant crowd think they can protect themselves by the power of talismans. I, too, believe in talismans (I may even believe more in them than other people do), but my belief is quite different. I believe talismans are powerful only if you are working psychically and physically in harmony with what they represent, with what they contain in the form of powers and virtues, because then you are reinforcing and nourishing these qualities. If a talisman is impregnated with purity and if you want it to be

efficacious, you must live a pure life; if it is impregnated with strength, you must live so that
this strength is nourished and so on. However, if
you rely on the talisman doing all the work without your harmonizing with its properties then,
in time, those properties will leave it and your
talisman will die. A talisman is powerful only
when it is sustained by your way of living.

III

Modern medicine has induced very bad habits; it has taught people that whatever their headaches, liver troubles or stomachaches, they can always go to a chemist and find the appropriate pill to ease the pain. There are even pills to make you feel better when you are sad! Unfortunately, however, there are no pills in the spiritual life. Clairvoyance, magic powers, the virtues that make you an Initiate, all have to be developed by you yourself. Even if you turn to books, you will find that they only give you exercises to do. It is, of course, perfectly possible to find a charlatan who will promise you heaven and earth, his first step being to take all your money, and the second to disappear! You have no grounds for complaint, however; you wanted to get powers by cheating and so cheating came to you.

A true Master will give you all the methods, but it is up to you to do the work that will allow you to obtain what you want. He cannot do the work for you, and it would be useless if he did. If you want to keep a spiritual gift, or a psychic power, you have to put in your own inner work, make your own efforts. A Master can open doors for you, but it is up to you to walk through them. He will never push you but when he sees that you have gone through that door, he will open more for you. Each time the Master sees that you are making progress, he will give you a harder task to achieve. However, most people are like children who always want to be carried; they are afraid and so do nothing to surpass themselves. They fear perfection which, though they desire it, they will never achieve, because there are still too many confused ideas within.

Stop expecting instant enlightenment; stop waiting for someone to wave a magic wand over you or lay his hands on you whilst saying a few magic phrases. Nobody, not even your Master, who is near to you, is going to do it. Stop waiting for miracles. The greatest miracles are already there around you, every minute of the day. People always want dramatic events, but even if these events happen, those who witness them forget them very quickly. In the past many Initiates performed miracles, and, of course, for a short while people were tremendously impressed, yet the miracles did not stop them from continuing to amuse themselves or committing crimes.

For example, Jesus performed miracles before the astonished multitudes.... But not long after they had welcomed him in triumph to Jerusalem crying, "Hosanna to the Son of David," they were shouting, "Crucify him." So you see the effect of miracles often is only to amuse the public. Miracles, for me, are sunrises, flowers opening, a child smiling or an insect making its way through tall grass; stars are miraculous, man and the way he is formed is a miracle... but the greatest of all miracles is the transformation of the human heart. Why do I think that? Because it is the hardest of things to do.

Everybody has to make his own efforts for transformation because transformation is never going to come automatically from the outside. Hindus say, "When the disciple is ready, the Master comes." This is a very profound statement, for it shows that it is always the disciple who has to make the efforts to attract the help he needs. Once he has made the efforts, it is absolutely certain that help will come. There is a universal law of love and mutual aid, but it cannot be set into motion unless you yourself have made efforts.

Stop waiting for miracles which you think your Master ought to do for you. Get rid of this attitude and then you will really start making progress and your Master will be able to help you effectively. This may seem odd to you, but in fact when you concentrate on someone, expecting him to do everything, you paralyse him. He can do nothing for you and you remain sterile. So get to work, prepare yourself and, the moment you need it, you will be helped. The same process can be seen in alchemy: as soon as the material which has been patiently, slowly worked over by the alchemist is ready, the universal spirit can descend to give it life and then, with a very little quantity of this matter, the alchemist can turn all metals into gold.

Christians are so proud of Jesus, "Our Lord Jesus... no one is as mighty as He!" Yes, but Jesus is Jesus and they... what are they? They are lazy weak people who do nothing to become like Jesus. It is not enough to rejoice that Jesus was a divinity. The greatness of Jesus does not authorize Christians to remain miserable wretches; they, too, must try to copy him.

What I say is not only true for Christians, but for Muslims, Buddhists and Jews. They are all proud of their teachers, Mohammed, Buddha and Moses and their sacred books. It does not seem to matter to them that they themselves are weak, dark and evil; because they belong to a mighty religion, they can strut about, glorying in that. You have only to look at the way Christians celebrate the birth of Jesus: it is such an extraordinary event that they must celebrate it by having gargantuan meals and getting drunk! Jesus, of course, is enchanted and proud to see his birth celebrated by behaviour that is diametrically opposed to his Teaching.

The time has come when man must stop counting on the greatness of his religion and its founders and only be concerned with the quality of his own life. Of course, he should draw strength from the Initiates and the sacred books, as that is not only normal, it is also desirable; but he can no longer proclaim the virtues of his religion whilst remaining at the most mediocre of levels.

I know many of you say, "We have the most remarkable Master, he does this and he does that..." but you do nothing at all about improving yourselves. I am not terribly pleased that people should cite me in this way whilst doing absolutely nothing to imitate my actions or adopt my point of view. Many brothers and sisters think my way of doing things is my affair, and they will carry on doing what suits them. They display my photograph everywhere, they state they have the greatest, most wonderful and best of Masters, are prepared to come to blows in support of their claims, yet they do nothing about imitating my attitude or my philosophy. A Master is only there to be glorified, not to be imitated. My God, what a mentality! You cannot deny the truth of what I have said, so from now on, will you stop praising me and do the much better thing of observing and applying my ideas?

It is time to stop behaving like children. What is the point of having a Master if you go on living however you please? You insist that your Master should be spotless and think that is enough. I know that if I committed the slightest fault, you would be furious and would leave me saying that I had deceived you because I no longer fitted your picture of an Initiate or a Master. You insist that I be irreproachable whereas you can do whatever you like. You put Initiates in a world apart; it is a very honorific position for them and they are most flattered, but it would be so much better if you decided to enter into their world because then you would feel obliged to change your way of living. You think that Initiates are very pure, very noble, and indeed they are, but what about you? It is very important that you should be working in the same way too.

From now on, learn to demand from yourself what you demand from Initiates. Do you want them to be honest, to help you and not lead you astray? Well, ask the same things from yourself in your dealings with others.

I have been revealing truths over the years and if, each day, you start dwelling on these truths as if they were beings who have come to you from Heaven, you will find a whole new world open up before you. Never forget that the beings on high watch to see how you treat the truths a Master brings you. A Master is an envoy, an ambassador who represents a whole country – in this case Heaven – and the way you treat him shows how you regard the country which sent him. Heaven tells me what to say to you to help your evolution, and if you do not take what I say seriously, how can you convince Heaven of your respect and love? It cannot be done and Heaven, noticing your carelessness, will take away its help.

If you want Heaven to look kindly on you, you must begin at the beginning: you must take its ambassadors seriously. You have no idea how many spirits are working through me to help you. Yes, thousands of entities have come to help you evolve and the consequences will not be good for you if you take all this lightly. I shall carry on with my work, whether you understand it or not; I will do it despite you and I will be the one who benefits. I would like you to benefit

also, but you must realize that this is not possible unless, firstly, you begin to understand how
many beings and forces are engaged in this work
of the great Universal White Brotherhood and,
secondly, you decide to change your life in order
to participate fully in this work.

8

THE DISCIPLE AND HIS MASTER

I

You must learn to make good use of the psychological method of polarization. When two people are polarized in the same way, the results are not good. Imagine a couple having an argument; the husband is shouting and waving his arms in anger; if his wife did the same they would end up killing each other. She should be intelligent enough to polarize herself negatively, accepting everything without comment, saying smilingly, "Yes, darling; of course, sweetheart"; he will then calm down, realizing that he has gone too far and apologize.

This law of polarization can be seen in many fields. If a disciple starts arguing and talking when he goes to his Master instead of listening, he will make no progress. When a Master sees his disciple's attitude, he will not persist as he knows that you cannot pour water into a bottle that is already full. The liquid overflows onto the ground and is wasted. The intelligent disciple knows how to polarize himself: when he is near his Master, he becomes receptive, he listens to him and receives the truths which are given to him and so goes away a richer man.

However, a disciple must not go to his Master with the sole intent of getting his Master's knowledge; he must also bring something to give. In case you are wondering what a disciple can give his Master, I will tell you.

Throughout the world, it is customary to bring a gift to the people you are visiting. It is a very ancient tradition, based on the principle that you must never go to someone with empty hands. You must always go with the desire to bring them something. I have often told you how important it is never to greet someone in the morning when you are holding an empty container, because you will bring him emptiness for the whole day. Do not think that this is a superstition which highly evolved men of the twentieth century should abandon. It is not a superstition, it is a law of the spiritual world which has often been verified.

Therefore, when you go to visit someone, make sure that you never arrive with an empty container, but also make sure that you come loaded with thoughts of all the most marvellous things such as fruit and flowers, gold, light and blessings. You must always get into the habit of giving, and of giving what is the best for every-one. Clearly this philosophy is not very wide-spread among people; most people have been taught how to take and, wherever they go, they think only of taking... they are interested only if they can make use of things for themselves. Even when they come to a Master and an Initiatic School, they only think of taking. After a while, as there is not much there for them to take ex-cept the truths which do not interest them great-ly, they get bored and off they go.

I will give you an exercise to do. Imagine that you have within you some wonderful land to be cultivated; see yourself as a garden full of all sorts of flowers and fruits and when you come here, bring the fruits of your garden to give to others. You cannot imagine what sensations you will feel. Because of this desire to do something for others, doors will open, everything will seem new and you will never stop making fresh dis-coveries, as giving to others makes life spring up within you.

So, therefore, when a disciple comes near his Master, he must long to bring the gifts of his soul and spirit. It is not enough to come just to re-ceive the Teaching, the wisdom and light of his Master; the disciple must bring something from within, in return, otherwise he will never see or understand anything and will go away as weak

and mediocre as he arrived. In the East, when a
disciple goes to see a Master, he never goes with
empty hands, he brings at least a fruit or a flower. Of course the Master has no need of it, but
this tradition teaches the disciple that he must
not expect everything from his Master. What a
disciple must bring his Master is not so much a
fruit or a flower, but a highly elevated state of
awareness, because only at that moment will he
be able to benefit from the wealth of the Teaching.

II

Some people come here with a very personal, even anarchic, attitude. However, I have a particular language, and it is you who must conform with me. I have a tuning fork which gives me the note, and if you want us to play a piece of music together, you must tune yourself to my note, not I to yours, because you are all tuned differently and if I were to harmonize with first one and then another, we would never get anywhere. If I had to conform to the tastes, the hopes, the plans, desires and whims of each one, it would take centuries before harmony could be installed. When I tuned in to one person's wavelength, I would be out of harmony with everyone else. Were I to harmonize with first one, and then another, would you all have the patience to wait for your turn? With too many different wavelengths, it would be like a hundred radio stations talking at once: what bedlam!

So I have hit on a very simple solution: if

everyone tunes in to the same wavelength, then
everything will work out perfectly. Even you will
feel the results; when you leave here, you will
feel that you vibrate quite differently and that
you no longer have any worries or cares. It is up
to you all to decide to harmonize on one wavelength: mine. Does that mean that I want to
monopolize you, hypnotize and enslave you?
Not at all. When you are at home, vibrate on all
the wavelengths you want; you are free to sing,
shout, scream as much as you want and no one
has the right to hinder you. Since, however, you
have chosen to come here, in the interest of collective harmony, choose also to harmonize with
me and you will find this is the best, the most ef-
fective and the most economical attitude to take.
Whilst you are here, speak my language.

If you decide to put yourself in harmony with
me, you will be the one to benefit. I say this, not
because I want to have you under my spell, or to
dominate you, but because it is in your best interest; if you all attune to my vibrations, my
ideas, my thoughts, you will get much more benefit from your stay here. You know that my sole
concern is to be useful to you; I have no other
desire. When I come here, I spend all my time
working for you. Even when I say nothing to
you, I speak to you from within, and I explain
all that you need to know. I always want to see

you happy, at peace, because it makes me happy to see others happy. I am very sad when I do not manage to please you, but when I see you happy and shining, I go home satisfied and thank the Lord.

If you are not afraid to get on to the same wavelength as me, you will benefit, because as I have said, my one wish is to be useful to you. So then, when we are together, even in silence, if you are plugged into my wavelength, you have much more chance of catching my thoughts, and receiving some of the particles which I send through space... and you are the one who gains. Those who have verified this over the years are absolutely convinced that this attitude, this agreement, this harmony has marvellous results on them.

When you are on the same wavelength, when you have the same thoughts, the same feelings, the same concerns as I do, you will make new discoveries, you will pick up new vibrations and as I am only a conductor (I do not wish to be anything but a conductor so that the divine world can help you through me), your cares, regrets, vexations, problems and torments will disappear. With all my heart I long for this for you.

In an orchestra or a choir, everybody has to respect the score, the beat and the nuances indicated by the conductor. No singer or musician has the right to do what he wants as otherwise there would be an appalling cacophony. An orchestra or a choir is a symbol of the harmony which must reign between people, a harmony which, unfortunately, we see hardly anywhere. Everybody thinks they should do what suits them personally rather than thinking of harmonizing with others. This state of disharmony is so widespread, so popular throughout the world that even when people go to an Initiatic School, they continue cultivating this anarchic attitude. Everybody comes intent on their own ideas whilst the poor teacher is left standing there by himself, looking at the chaos all around.

From now on, you must understand that a teacher is like a conductor; he is there to see that harmony rules, and that is why everyone must synchronize with him. He is the tuning fork and when all are in tune, they will make the most marvellous music, like harps swept by the wind. The teacher is the essential tuning fork and disciples must learn to understand that the only purpose of an instructor is to introduce and maintain harmony. There will be no progress whilst everyone sits in their corners doing whatever they please.

Let this be quite clear: if the disciple has to tune in with his Master, it is because the Master himself is capable of tuning in with universal life, with divine life. The only concern of a Master is that each day, several times a day, he should put himself in harmony with Heaven, vibrating in unison with it so that he is then able to communicate this harmony to his disciples.

Therefore I am a tuning fork for you, and if you want to vibrate in harmony with the heavenly world, try to harmonize with the philosophy I am bringing you, otherwise, even if you spend your whole life in an Initiatic School, you will make no progress. You have come here of your own free will (I have not taken you by the throat and dragged you here), but if you have no desire to harmonize with me, your stay here will be quite useless and you would be better off elsewhere, amusing yourself. You see, you are not even clear on the reason for coming to the Fraternity. I have harmonized myself with other beings who surpass me and if you learn to vibrate on the same wavelength as I do, you will see your whole life transformed. I link myself ceaselessly to higher beings so that I will not commit an error, or do anything harmful for you, because I realize that I am responsible for you.

I feel that some of you come here with a feeling of distrust; even though you are not aware of it, you are afraid of losing your liberty, your independence and of becoming weak. You think to yourselves, "After all, you never know, a

Master could hypnotize you, put you under his spell and make use of you any way he likes." In fact, you have no idea how aware a true Master is of his responsibilities; he knows that he will have to answer to Heaven for each and every action. You are not the most important thing for him; Heaven takes the first place. I would even say that you are no more for me than my workshop. Forgive me for saying so, but it is true. I take time over you, I teach you, I guide you, because Heaven has given me this job, but whilst I am working I think not of you but of the heavenly beings whom I must satisfy.

So rejoice over this state of affairs, because if it were the opposite, if I were concerned only with you and not with the heavenly beings, I would have made many mistakes with you. However, since I have never abandoned the thought that there exist higher beings to whom I shall one day have to render account, you are the ones to benefit. If I were to forget those beings in order just to think of you, despite myself, I would have made very serious errors. It is inevitable that once you have cut the link with Heaven, you cannot but do wrong. You must not count on human intelligence and human kindness alone; when they are not inspired by heavenly intelligence and heavenly kindness, they can only lead you over precipices.

So do not be irritated if I tell you that you do not matter very much for me. In fact, rejoice! The important thing for you is not to know if you count or not, but to feel whether you become richer, stronger, wiser and happier. If that is the case, there is no need to bother about the rest. The one thing to understand is that inasmuch as you work with me and inasmuch as I have the responsibility to teach you true knowledge, leading you along the right path by giving you what I myself have received, you do matter a great deal to me.

I hope that from now on you will come towards me with much more confidence. I have no desire at all to control you or injure you. Not, I repeat, because you are so important to me but because I know I will have to answer for my acts to those who cannot be deceived. If you come with a receptive and confident attitude, I can write great truths in your soul. It will be done without your realizing it, but one day, when you least expect it, when you are walking down the street or sitting at home, you will suddenly be struck by a truth that has come down to your conscious level and you will be dazzled by its beauty.

9

THE UNIVERSAL DIMENSION
OF A MASTER

You must not come to the Fraternity for me, but for the Teaching, which is rich, vast and infinite. If you come because one day I gave you a smile, you will leave if the time comes when, for one reason or another, I fail to give you one. Smiles are not the essential thing. A Master is so busy, even overburdened, that he does not always have time to smile. The disciple must not expect everything to come from him otherwise he will end up losing not only his Master but the Teaching. What on earth can a Master do with someone who is only attached to his person but not to his ideas? He can sense that his disciple wants only to monopolize him, absorb him and, knowing how dangerous that is, he will do all he can to distance himself and escape from such a clutching disciple. Whereas if he sees the disciple has come for the Teaching, he will support him and help him so that this intelligent disciple will gain both the Teaching and his Master. You see, it is quite clear, if you want to get nearer to me, really apply yourself to the Teaching.

I have received many letters in my life from women who had undeniably good qualities, but they also had a most bizarre idea in their heads: more than anything, they wanted to marry me! It was no use telling them that I was already married, that the Universal White Brotherhood was both my fiancée and my wife; it had no effect. I explained this very nicely (although sometimes it made me quite angry), but they could not understand my attitude. Frankly, I tell you that when I see certain brothers and sisters attach themselves only to my person, I am afraid because I know all the complications that will arise from this, and so I do everything to distance myself from them. How can I make them understand that what they want is not only dangerous but impossible?

When you have learnt to read and decipher the living book of nature, you understand that if order and harmony reign throughout the universe, it is quite simply because the sun is there in the centre, and in the centre he stays. That is why an Initiate, a Master, who is responsible for the evolution of so many people, must have a little conversation with the sun from time to time. "Listen, dear sun, there are so many people who love me and want to draw me over to their direction. What do you advise me to do?" The sun will reply, "Look at me and see how I behave. The planets love me very much too, they revolve around me, but I stay right there in the centre. I do not move towards one or another, even though they may say, 'Oh darling sun, if I could only nestle up to you, if I could only embrace you.... Do come near me....' I think about it and see that I, too, love them, maybe even more than they love me; the love of all these united planets could not be compared with the immensity of my love, because in my love, there is no personal motive, just light, warmth and life. In order to look after their well-being, I am forced to keep my place and not go towards them, as otherwise there would be a universal cataclysm. You see, I must stay where I am at the centre, in order to maintain harmony, life and happiness throughout the universe. So why don't you do exactly as I do? There's nothing to stop you loving everybody, giving them light, inspiring them, uplifting them and leading them towards heavenly regions, but you must not leave the centre." "Yes, but they keep asking me!" "Oh my goodness me," the sun will reply, "if you are going to spend all your time satisfying the desires and whims of everybody, the whole thing will collapse!"

An Initiatic School is like a solar system: you find in it many planets and, unfortunately, you also find comets which are attracted in and then sweep off into the distance.... And the Master, who is at the centre like the sun, must stay at the centre. He gives his strength, his warmth, his light, his blessings, his ideas, but he does not shift from his central place. Some masters, who did not know that their decision could provoke a real catastrophe, took one of their disciples as a wife, whereupon the other disciples, seeing that their Master had got married, left him. Masters who act like that are therefore not true suns; symbolically, they are more like moons, as the moon is more open to influences, more unstable, more sentimental, more drawn to the earth. There have been several moons already in our solar system; continents are moons which have fallen to earth. Perhaps you do not believe me, but all this is written in the archives of Initiatic Science.

All Initiates who have this lunar side (by which I mean an emotional and sentimental side) highly developed, are attracted by people, and they change their position by leaving the centre. However, true suns think and ponder and then stay where they are. This does not mean that they are cold, frozen and egotistical, not at all. They give their love, their light and their strength but they keep their place at the centre. Even when confronted by the most beautiful of girls, even princesses, they will stay motionless, saying, "I will send you rays of light, I will give you my affection, but let me stay in the place where I am."

Just by drawing near to the Teaching which I bring you means that you will be with me all the time. When I see a soul working for the light, I am attracted by it as moths are by the light of a candle. This is the sole condition; the soul must be working for the light! If it is not, neither promises nor menaces will make me yield. I love light, beauty, and purity: if you work on these qualities, I will be working ceaselessly with you, my thoughts will be with you to support you, to help and protect you. If I see that you wish to monopolize me for yourself, without leaving anything for others, I become fearful of such egoism and lack of understanding and so do all I can to escape you. You should not be coming here in order to monopolize me but to learn and to work.

As long as you look for me merely on the physical plane, you must realize that I will never be able to satisfy you because I do not have enough time to spend with you. When I meet you, I can give you a nut, a pistachio, a sweet or

a smile and that is all.... But if you climb higher
into the realm of thought and spirit I can be concerned with your well-being; each moment of
the day and night you will receive something.
An Initiate, knowing how to work with thought,
is able to create currents of forces on the higher
planes and so he can be everywhere throughout
the universe, penetrating plants, oceans and
stars with his quintessence. You may think that
this is enormous pride and vanity. You are free
to think what you want but I am telling you the
truth.

If you look for me on the physical plane, I
cannot do much for you, but if you look for me
in higher regions, you will feel that I never stop
thinking about you. How do I do it? That is my
business, but there is nothing else which interests me except this task of being concerned with
you and with many others whom you do not
know. If you do not feel that you are receiving
anything, it is because you are closed; you have
not learned to climb into luminous regions in
order to understand that I am concerned only
with feeding you on the most substantial elements. I tell you this in all humility and simplic-
ity: I never stop working for you in other regions. Other luminous beings also work for
you... for a Master, a true Master, who is aware
of the value of divine work, is always linked to

Heaven. Even when he has to leave to do other work, he always stays linked to his Fraternity.

For this reason, in times of absence, there are always other entities of the invisible world which manifest, representing him, in order to maintain and support the collectivity.

The disciple will never lose anything if he has confidence and loves his Master. He will always be supported, helped, enlightened and vivified, if not by the Master himself, by others who are always linked to him and who are always there. Many have verified this fact; when I was busy elsewhere, when I was not even aware of their difficulties, they were helped. They thought that it came from me, but it was not I who helped them, but my friends in the invisible world who acted in my place. They are not proud or vain and so they do not mind taking my face to appear before you. As for me, I am the last one to know what has been happening.

Some time ago, I received a letter from a physicist, a researcher at CNRS (The National Institute for Scientific Research) who said, "O Master, what clarity, what light I find in your books! I have known many spiritual movements, and I have read many esoteric books, but I have never found the basic problems dealt with with such lucidity. I would like to meet you, but

only you, as I do not like collective living. Will
you receive me?" So what do you think I should
say to him? It would be better for him not to
come, because he is not ready. I do not want
people here who are interested only in our ideas
just so that they can make use of them in their
own selfish ways. I need people who like the collectivity and who long to join in a communal
work to bring the Kingdom of God on earth.
That is why, when some bluntly tell me that
they do not like the collectivity and that they
only wish to meet me, I always ask myself what
they would do with what I tell them. I do not
care to receive such people; I am very honoured
by the fact that they want to make the effort to
meet me, but I have no need for such egoists.
They can go where they like, but they cannot
come here!

I would even go further. If I decided not to
give any more conferences, not to tell you anything more, that would not be a reason for you
to stop coming to the Fraternity. One does not
come to a spiritual Teaching just to gather up a
lot of facts as one does at school and university,
thinking that once the course is finished, the stu-
dents leave their teachers.

You do indeed come to learn something
here, but this knowledge should stimulate you to
work. The work is for all of us together to make

an extraordinarily powerful battery; yes, hundreds of united souls and spirits produce magical waves of an extraordinary power which can enlighten and help people who are plunged deep in shadows and sufferings.... Until the day comes when we will finally be able to bring the Kingdom of God on earth. Do not make me your goal, or the gaining of knowledge your goal, but do your spiritual work for the good of humanity as this work lasts throughout eternity.

10

THE MAGICAL PRESENCE OF A MASTER

When I was a disciple of Master Peter Deunov, I was very poor; I had nothing but a bed, a violin and a few books. I spent weeks in the mountains, reading and meditating. From time to time, I took a job in order to earn a little money. If you had only seen the shoes and the clothes which I wore! Yet I was happy because I felt rich, fabulously rich; I felt that my head and my heart contained all the wealth of the universe, because I had a Master. I felt that because of him, I would achieve all the most precious things I longed for.

If I told you my state of happiness and joy at that time when I met my Master, you would not believe me. That state is still with me today. You may object, "You no longer need a Master as you, yourself, are a Master." Even if I am a Master, even if I were to become the greatest of them all, I assure you that I would always have the same respect and the same love for all Masters.

Here in the West, people have no idea what a Master can do in guiding the direction of their destiny, of all that his presence can do for them in order to improve, guide, rectify and harmonize them. The idea of a Master is not attractive to them because they know that he will not leave them in peace with their follies, he will show them the danger of the path they are on and, obviously, that would make them feel a little uneasy, which they would not want at all.

Besides, there is no point in our having any illusions. Even should they find a Master and apparently accept him, they will still prefer all sorts of trivial futilities to him. The Master will only be a decorative frill on their lives. What they really think is that he is merely a servant there to obey them; they are the real masters and their Master, poor wretch, is just there to satisfy their whims. If the Master should dare to say something which fails to please his disciples, watch out for their reactions!

Only Orientals really know how to appreciate the value of a Master. They need a Master in order to stimulate them, to inspire them and to link them to Heaven, and when they have found him, they neither have doubts about him nor dispute with him. He is a path which will allow them to reach the heights. Their Master may not even have talked to them, he may not even have noticed them, but they know he exists and so they are happy, progressing because they love him, believe in him and are linked to him. When they are unhappy, ill, poor and dying, they feel consoled and comforted merely by the thought he exists; with this thought in their hearts and minds they overcome all difficulties. Knowing that he exists makes them evolve, advance, learn and become strong, because this image is within and is all-powerful. This inner Master opens doors to them, often without the physical Master knowing anything of them and their problems.

Brothers and sisters have told me many times, "I was ill and going through terrible difficulties. I called to you, you came, you talked to me and then everything that you said to me came true." This kind of story amazes me: I had no idea of all this; how could it have happened without my knowing anything?

The disciple carries his Master within himself, in his head and soul and it is that Master who is so powerful and able to help, console and heal him. What am I capable of doing? When people come and tell me what has happened to them, I am astonished. I say to myself, "This Master they carry in their heads is remarkable, he can do miracles which are beyond my capabilities." Therefore, you see, what matters is not

so much the Master himself as what you think,
believe and imagine about him. If you had an
all-powerful, all knowing Master in front of you
and you did not believe in him, thinking that he
was ignorant, weak and feeble, he would never
be able to help you. Why is that? Because the
only thing that matters is your way of looking at
him, your faith in him and nothing else.

If you were to say, "I want to meet the greatest Master so that he can teach me," I would
tell you that you had formulated the wrong desire. You might be able to meet him, but if you
had not already worked on how to understand a
Master, how to love him, how to appreciate
what he is teaching you, were you to meet the
greatest Master on earth, you would disagree
with him and would remain as stupid as before.

It is the quality of your thoughts and feelings
which help you to progress and the Master is
only a means to get there. All those who think
that their spiritual evolution would be made easier if they had a great Master, or an even greater
Master, are mistaken; the one certainty is that
they would have greater tests. Do not imagine
that if a cat came near to Jesus he would become
St. John! The cat will stay a cat and the pig may
become even more piggish!

Obviously it is good to have a Master who is
wise and full of love, but never forget that the

most important thing is yourself, because when you have something good, wondrous and divine within, it always ends up attracting corresponding elements. Therefore even were I not able, according to your way of looking at it, to help you as you would like, that does not matter. If you are sincere and if you believe that others can work through me to help you, you will never be deceived. The essential element is yourself. So begin to improve your thoughts and your feelings, knowing that sooner or later, by the law of affinity, you will attract the elements that correspond to your thoughts.

Think about what a Master can represent in your inner life – not your outer life but your inner one – what a powerful transformer he can be in the head of the disciple who believes in him. When I was in India, I heard this anecdote; it is without doubt a legend, but it is very significant. A Master had a young boy amongst his disciples who loved him so much that he never stopped repeating his name as a magic formula. He did this so much that one day, in his love and faith, he began to walk upon the water. Somebody told the Master of the miracle and so he called his disciple to him saying, "People have been telling me the most extraordinary things about you. Apparently you walk on water. How do you do it?" "Oh Master," replied the disciple, "I just said your name with love." The Master said to himself that he, too, could do the same, so he went to the river, stepped on the water, pronounced his own name and drowned! He drowned, whilst his disciple walked on the water. It is not so much the name that was important, as the intensity with which the disciple pronounced it. If his Master had had himself an even higher Master for whom he felt the same love and the same confidence, he, too, could have walked on the water, just like his disciple.

Therefore, whatever heights you have reached, you must never stop there; you must always love and serve a higher being than yourself, so that you can, thanks to him, perform miracles and do good. Otherwise, you will drown whilst others will perform all the miracles. The Indian Master of the story did not know much about true spiritual laws.

With all my heart, I shall always go on loving and respecting all the great Masters of humanity; even if I were to surpass them, I would continue to admire them, because I know that it is my respect that brings me everything, not the Masters themselves. It may be that they do not even know that I exist and that they give me nothing, but my love and my respect for them give me everything and so I will walk on the water; just because of this respect and this love.

11

IDENTIFICATION

II

IDENTIFICATION

I

When two people love each other, there are exchanges between them and their auras intermingle. For this reason, when you are with a great Master whom you love and with whom you communicate, there are also exchanges and your aura is purified, strengthened and enlarged. Here lies the usefulness of loving very elevated, very evolved beings : even when you love great Masters who are no longer on earth (Jesus, Buddha, Krishna, Zoroastra), there is a sort of osmosis that goes on between you and the Master and so you benefit from his light. If you are lucky enough to be near a living Master, to be right there in his aura, to be permeated with it, that, of course, is even better.

When disciples concentrate on their Master, they receive his emanations of purity and light, but what do they give him? Believe me, the exchange is not all that wonderful for the Master, for he receives only dirt and filth in exchange for all his gifts. As he has accepted the need to make sacrifices and as he has learnt to transform the impurities he receives, he tolerates the situation, does not complain, and in this way he helps his disciples.

The disciple who has made efforts to identify with his Master creates a magical link between the two of them and with the help of this link, he begins, little by little, to resemble his Master. He may not look like him physically (even though with much willpower, faith and time this can happen), but within, he will receive the wisdom and the light of this Master. I understood when I was still very young how useful it was for me to identify with my Master. Nobody, not even he, had told me to do it, it was as if I could remember the value of identification from some distant past. I wanted to enter into his spirit and I imagined that I could think like him, feel like him and act like him. I did this without saying anything to anybody, not even to him, and years afterwards, not only had I begun to think like him but also even to look like him physically. I gained a great deal from this exercise. I felt that if I stayed like most other people where I was, I would not get very far. I wanted to replace all my imperfections with the qualities and the virtues of all the great Masters, and it was this attitude which allowed me to make progress.

If you try to talk to people about replacing their limited mentality, see how they react! They guard it, protect it, cling on to it and that is why you can see on their faces the traces of the disorders and torments that they experience. Their lives are made up of shabby tricks, divisions, arguments and difficulties caused by their lower nature, which they are not willing to alter. How many times have I told you at the Michaelmas fire ceremony to learn to decipher what was happening before your eyes. Those branches which made the fire were black and twisted and yet look at the splendid fire they have produced! So why do you go on clutching your old dead branches, instead of sacrificing them so that they too can be transformed into heat and light. The word "sacrifice" makes people shudder, they are so terrified of losing something and this is understandable, but without sacrifice they will have neither warmth nor light.

This fear of sacrificing their lower nature makes people ignore the essential truths which could have saved them. When they are told to enter the spirit of their teacher, their Master, they feel that such an exercise would take away their freedom and their power whereas, in fact, the effect is quite the opposite: to identify with a Master who surpasses you, will help you to even greater liberty and powers. Of course this takes place only if the Master is someone who surpasses you; otherwise, it is useless.

This exercise of identification is based on the knowledge of a physical law, the law of resonance. If you vibrate in unison with a particular being, not only do you know his thoughts and his feelings but his qualities are communicated to you. Otherwise, however much you study him, judge him and categorize him, in reality you will not truly know him because you will only know him from the outside. Real knowledge comes when you vibrate in unison with him. Being on the same wavelength as someone draws you together so that you can know each other. True love is true knowledge, because true love is nothing other than a fusion.

The disciple who wishes to become like his Master must therefore try to introduce the same vibrations into himself. It is entirely a question of vibrations. You can even become greater than your Master, depending on the quality of your love; the one with the greatest love always becomes the greater. Knowledge and strength are obviously important but these do not take one the farthest; it is with love that one goes right to infinity. Love makes you run, so that you never stop. Love makes you take to your heels! Any love which allows you to stagnate is not true love.

Once upon a time, in a far away country, there was a young man who had exceptional strength and he decided to put this strength at the service of the most powerful man on earth. So he went to serve a king in a neighbouring country who took him as his personal body-guard. One day the king and his entourage were crossing a forest where they had been warned that they would be passing close by a spot haunted by the Devil. The king therefore gave the order for a detour. "Aha," said the lad, "what's all this? The king cannot be the most powerful man in the world if he is afraid of someone called the Devil." So he left the king and went to look for the Devil so that he could serve him.

One evening he saw a great band of sinister-looking black knights. "What are you looking for?" said the leader. "I am looking for the Devil." "I am he," replied the Devil, "what do you wish with me?" "I was in the service of the most powerful king on earth but I saw one day that he was afraid of you. You are therefore more powerful than he, and so I wish to serve you." "Fine, that's agreed, come with us." So he followed the Devil. One day he noticed that the band of black knights avoided a spot where there were crosses; he asked what there was about the crosses that made the knights avoid them. History does not relate what the Devil told the young man about

Jesus, but he understood that Jesus must be even more powerful than the Devil as the Devil was afraid of Him. So once again, he decided to leave in search of the more powerful one. He looked for a long time; many days and nights passed without achieving his goal. So he set himself up by the side of a river as a ferryman. He was so big and strong that he carried the travellers on his shoulders from one side to the other, supporting his steps through the river by leaning on a great staff.

One night, when he was in his little hut, a terrible storm burst, with thunder and lightning and the rain flooding down in torrents. He could not sleep and as he lay there, he heard the faint cry of a weeping child. Astonished, he went out of the hut, and there, in the darkness, he could make out the form of a very small child. "My dear little one, what are you doing here in such weather?" "I would like to cross the river, but I cannot as I am too small!" "Stop crying and I will carry you across," said the ferryman. He lifted him onto his shoulders and stepped into the river. But the waters rose so high and the current was so strong that he made little progress, particularly as he could feel that the child on his shoulders was growing heavier and heavier.... "Why are you so heavy, my child?" asked the ferryman. "You weigh more than the earth itself!" The child replied, "Oh yes, I am heavier than the earth. I am Jesus whom you wished to serve. From this day forward you will be called Christopher, the Christ bearer."

That is the legend of St. Christopher and if the disciple, like Christopher, leaves a weak and cowardly Master for a powerful and fearless Master, who can blame him? If he wants to serve the greatest Master, he is in no way guilty. The greatest and most powerful Master is the sun. Compared with him, all others are weak, sickly and unsteady. The only one who can resist all storms and tempests is the sun. As he is the strongest, he is the one we should serve and from whom we should learn. However, people who have not received Initiatic Science have not yet started to understand things in this way. Even talking about vibrating in unison with the soul and spirit of their Master is beyond their understanding, so how much more so when I speak of the sun!

True magic for the disciple is, therefore, to be able to identify with his Master so that he can touch all there is in the soul, the heart, the intelligence and the will of the Master so that then all these treasures will pour on him. A Master is not selfish and greedy, he wants to give abundantly. Should he see that one of his disciples surpasses him, he is proud of him saying, "That's my

child, he is more intelligent than I; he is better
than I; he is stronger than I; all the better, because I am his father." A father who is furious
because his son surpasses him is not a true
father. If a Master is furious that his disciple has
surpassed him, if he is jealous and begins to harass him and torment him, that shows that he
has not yet arrived at the highest degree of disinterestedness which is the greatest quality of a
Master. Indeed there are Masters who have not
got rid of jealousy.

You must never blame a disciple who wants
to surpass his Master. If God has given you these
qualities, what is to hinder you from developing
them? What you should be aiming for, your
ideal goal, is to be like God Himself rather than
to be like your father, your mother or your Master. A Master is a way, a stage, a gateway, a
teacher, a father, for a certain time, but nowhere
is it written that you should stop and put down
roots beside your Master. What is written is that
you must go towards God through your Master.
Where can you find a more sensible, more utterly true idea? I am not interested in whether you
make up ideas to suit yourselves; my job always
is to give you the most truthful, most luminous
and most heavenly of ideas.

A Master is like a father or a mother who
brings you up, but you should not stay always

beside your mother and father; you must go towards God. Now, if your Master has reached God, you will be with him, next to God, and that will be even better. Otherwise, one should not stay eternally beside one's Master. In fact a Master does not stay on the same spot, he evolves rapidly; so you must walk with him and you may even have to run! He is going towards God, he is not going to stay beside you and you must run with him so that you, too, may get near God. Why? Because the goal of all beings is God... and the starting point is God also.

You ask, "What about my father and my mother?" They are contractors who built your body, your house, whether it be a hut or a temple. "But I want them to come with me!" Very well, try to sweep them along in your wake!

II

Many of you wonder how I manage to explain certain passages in the Gospels which have never been explained over the last two thousand years. For example, what did Jesus mean when He said, "My Father works and I work with Him"? What kind of work was he talking about? "Ask, and it shall be given you; seek, and ye shall find; knock, and it shall be opened unto you"? For what are we seeking, asking, knocking? Then there are the parables, the unjust steward, the five wise and the five foolish virgins, the camel which can pass through the eye of a needle whereas a rich man cannot enter the gate to the Kingdom of God.... Perhaps Jesus gave explanations to his disciples, but they were not recorded in the Gospels. So how are we to know exactly what he wanted to say?

When I was very young, I asked myself this question and I read many books where the words of Jesus were discussed, but I was never really satisfied with their explanations. One day, after much reflection, I had this revelation that I should work on getting into the mind of Jesus and so I began to work with my imagination. God has given man this extraordinary faculty whereby he can picture to himself the things that he cannot possess or do on the physical plane and thus create the conditions for realizing them. Unfortunately man uses this faculty only to satisfy his lowest instincts : his sensuality, his desire for possession, for domination and vengeance. What people are able to imagine in these areas is almost unbelievable! That is why the imagination must now be taught to work for heavenly activities.

Therefore, in order to enter into the mind of Jesus, I imagined that I was in Palestine, in all the places that the Gospel mentioned (the towns, the mountains, the river Jordan or the lake of Genesaret) and I said to my disciples all the phrases whose meanings I wanted to understand. I imagined in this way that I was right in the consciousness of Jesus and that I saw, thought and felt like him. Obviously I did not achieve this all in one day. I worked for a long, long time at it. Sometimes I was successful and at others I was not. If I can now say that I am able to throw more light on the meaning of the parables in the Gospels than others, it is as a result of this exercise which I did over the years to enter the mind of Jesus.

Let us speak now in a more general fashion about this exercise. If you want to enter the mind of your instructor to understand his thoughts, you may succeed but only when your motives are pure, unselfish, and you ask only heavenly things. If you enter someone's mind, you bring him all the good and evil within yourself. Only to very advanced beings who are capable of transforming all the impurities you bring, can you do this without damage.

People are so far from understanding these truths! They never bother to find out if their thoughts and desires are going to disturb or soil others. When a man decides to walk on the path of spirituality, something beautiful, luminous and powerful is released from him. So, as women are sensitive to this charm, they start imagining all sorts of things without thinking of all the temptations they are creating for this man on the invisible plane. Feminine nature is made this way, it cannot be made wise; from the moment a woman feels an impulse, she has to follow it. For this reason, many Initiates have succumbed because of the continual assault of women who want to make them fall in love with them. Only those who are really strong have been able to resist it. I am not saying that you should not love your Teacher. Yes, you should love him, but in a spiritual way in order to support him, to protect him, so that he may advance in his task.

If you want to enter the mind of an Initiate, it is better to choose a very great Master like Jesus or Hermes or Melchisedech, because even if you are the most imperfect of men, you will not risk harming them or hindering their work. This exercise that I did with Jesus I did with my Master, Peter Deunov also : but I did not do it lightly. It was only with respect and inspired by holy feelings that I dared enter the head of my Master. It is only when you feel respect and devotion that this exercise of entering the mind of an Initiate can be really useful and beneficial for you, for you then vibrate on the same wavelength as he does and thus you can explore the world of his thought.

12

"EXCEPT YE BECOME AS LITTLE CHILDREN..."

You may wonder why the invisible world sends children to be with adults and not with other children. It is so that they can find models in their parents as, without models, one cannot grow, learn and develop. However, parents are often pretty strange models! They are not always the perfect example they should be. As children instinctively copy their parents, if the parents are not quite as they should be, neither are the children. Adults themselves need a model which surpasses them, but they do not wish to acknowledge the truth of this; they think that they are impeccable and perfect and it is this very self-satisfaction that precipitates them towards catastrophes.

Do you think that I did not need to have models to attain all that I desired? Yes, indeed, and as I have not found perfect enough models here on earth, I look for them elsewhere in the divine world, and so I progress each day. It is only a little progress, of course, but advancing each day, over thousands of years, I have been able to cover an immense distance. Yes, I have enough patience to work over thousands of years.

So Heaven sends children to be near adults so that they can have models, but also so that the parents may have examples too. An adult is so heavy and stupid, whereas a child who smiles and laughs has doors opened to him immediately. If you think that after this explanation, everyone will decide from today to become as little children, you are mistaken. They will continue, as before, weighing themselves down with burdens, cares and complications, because they have understood nothing.

Why do I go on behaving like a child? Many who see me for the first time are astonished. "What is going on with this chap? We were told that we were going to meet a Master, and we are seeing a child who laughs and jokes, who waves his head and arms and legs about...." They have not understood that I want to keep my childhood within me. "But sometimes you are serious, deep and profound, like an old man!" "Ah well, that is in order to have a bit of variety!" The real truth is that I want my heart to remain a child's forever, always ready to love, to be enthusiastic, but that my intellect should be that of a man thousands of years old, full of wisdom and experience. So you see, both the child and the old man are always there in me, but each has his proper place, unlike many people who have a puerile intellect and an old, indifferent heart.

What happens with a small child? His parents look after him, feeding him, washing him and dressing him; he has nothing to worry about and no work to do. As for adults, the situation is the exact opposite, they have all the burdens, the complications and the obligations weighing them down: they have to find the money to deal with all the family's needs, to feed, house and protect them. I am, of course, speaking in general: I know perfectly well that some children are ill-treated, abandoned and thrown on to the streets by their parents and also that there are certain privileged rich people who spend their lives in peace and happiness. I am not dealing with these exceptions to the rule.

So if we are to look for the cause of this difference of situation between the child and the adult, we see that the child enjoys this protection because he is not capable of looking after himself. While he has not yet got the necessary faculties to provide for himself, to direct his life, he stays under the protection of his parents. Later on, when he feels strong and capable, he will take on responsibilities, he will want to work, dominate and test himself; and it is at this moment that the troubles begin, quite simply because he has to count on himself, his own faculties, strength and way of looking at things. So to be a child or an adult is not so much a question of age as one of attitude.

The thing that really interests me is to know how one should behave oneself in the spiritual life. Disciples and Initiates do not want to become masters of their own lives, to run them according to their own way of seeing things; they do not wish to cut the link with the Creator, they want to stay children. I mean by this that they want to obey their heavenly parents, by following them and doing everything according to their advice. Since they have this attitude, Heaven pays attention to them, feeding them, watching over them and protecting them. So here is a new interpretation for you of the words of Jesus, "Except ye become as little children, ye shall not enter in the kingdom of heaven." Because they have become adult, people feel strong, free and without any need of their Heavenly Father nor the Divine Mother; they cut their link with them. From that moment all miseries fall on them, Heaven pays them no attention: they are grown up! If they had continued to be children, not publishing their independence from Heaven, but feeling the need to be guided by Heaven, had followed its advice confidently, had walked along hand in hand with their divine parents, then Heaven would have continued to give them its attention and protection.

I am not saying that one should not become adult, but that whilst adult one should keep a child-like attitude towards Heaven, showing obedience, humility and love. When Heaven sees someone behave like this, it sends its help and its light. Heaven will only come to help you if you are a child. "But I am already an old man of ninety-nine!" That does not matter, sublime entities will pay no attention to your wrinkles, beard or white hair; they pay no attention to the official calendar; they see you are an adorable child, a child of God, and so they will let you enter paradise.

I have met many young people who have such great confidence in their own way of thinking, their knowledge and point of view, that they will not accept anyone's advice. They do not even listen to a Master. When I see this attitude, I know that difficulties lie ahead of them which they are not ready to meet or resolve correctly. They have an "adult" mentality: instead of being like children who are conscious of their ignorance and weakness, trusting in their parents and accepting their advice, they rely absolutely on their own opinions. These boys and girls have already become too old; they are heading for great disillusion and suffering.

If you ask, "How long do we have to go on keeping up this child-like attitude?" I answer, "Until you have become so pure and luminous that the Holy Spirit can come and live within you." When the Holy Spirit has come to live within a man, that is when he can really consider himself an adult. God has not made man in such a way that he should stay a child for eternity. These two stages, childhood and adulthood, have been foreseen by Cosmic Intelligence; we must be children for a certain length of time until we reach maturity. However, maturity is not where people have chosen to place it: when you are twenty-one or eighteen, you are no longer a minor, but you have not yet reached the majority I am discussing. Even at ninety-nine, many have not really reached their majority as they have no spiritual maturity.

When a person has received the Holy Spirit, he becomes truly adult; then he walks with the light and sees clearly. Only that adult is recognized as adult by Heaven. All others are merely recalcitrant children. Yes, all those who have not reached this spiritual maturity are regarded, on high, as babies. So this should now be clear to you. Man is not condemned to remain a child always, but until he has received the light, the

Spirit of God which brings all riches, he must keep the attitude of a child, by which I mean that he should always stay obedient, humble and attentive towards Heaven. When you see people caught up in inextricable difficulties, it is a clear proof that they are still disobedient children, because true adults no longer suffer: they are always in the light. All those who do not wish to keep this child-like attitude until their maturity, and who have become prematurely adult, are the ones who suffer.

So what is to be done? It is very simple: as you have not yet become adults, you must ask to be enlightened and guided by your heavenly parents. When they see that you are becoming stronger and stronger, more radiant, luminous and full of love, they will decide to give you your majority and then the spirit of light will never stop illuminating and inspiring you. Until you have been recognized as adult by Heaven, you must behave like a humble and obedient child so that you can enter the Kingdom of God.

There is one thing you must understand clearly. When I say that you must be humble and obedient, I mean towards the Lord... not towards people. Very often people have assumed that they should obey and submit to anybody and so they have been obedient towards tyrants, the wealthy, the powerful and executioners!

You should be faithful, devout, submissive and obedient only towards the divine principles.

Spiritual life allows periods of transformation which mark the passage from one stage to another, just as it occurs in puberty and the menopause on the physical and psychological planes. These passages do not show in quite such an apparent way on the spiritual plane, but they are very significant as they produce great changes in the inner life. As in physical life the child passes through adolescence to adulthood, so a similar passage is foreseen in our spiritual evolution. We must stay children until we have reached the maturity of an adult, but once an adult, there is no question of continuing to behave like a child.

"Except ye become as little children, ye shall not enter into the kingdom of heaven." These words are easy to understand. The day you stop trusting in the Heavenly Father and the Divine Mother, you stop loving them, that day you begin to feel the burdens, the misery and the ugliness of life; you are weary, you no longer have the gaiety of a joyful carefree child who plays and sings; you become wrinkled and withered, bowed down with the burdens you carry on your own shoulders. If, despite the duties and encumbrances you have as an adult, you always want to stay a heavenly child because you know that you have parents on high who love you, then you blossom and become beautiful, smiling and luminous.

Is that quite clear now? We all have nothing else to do except to become the children of Heaven, for in feeling the love of our Father and our Mother, their presence and their help, we will be sustained, protected, encouraged and enlightened, ceaselessly. Those who think that they are already strong enough to allow themselves to cut the link with Heaven feel miserable and abandoned in the coldest solitude. When you see a man overburdened, crushed with care, you can say, "That man became a premature adult; he should have stayed a child."

Realize that you have an interest in approaching a Master as often as possible to obtain this new way of seeing things. In the same way that you need a father, you need a Master, for a Master is another form of father. "It is not necessary, I already have a father!" Yes, but can he teach you all you will learn from a Master?

In all the initiations of the past the same thing was taught then as is taught now. There are three beings whom the disciple needs to love and respect if he is to advance on the evolutionary path: in order to fulfill his need for divine love, the Heavenly Father; to learn the meaning of universality, the sun; and to enlighten his intelligence, a Master.

By the same author:

"Complete Works" Collection

Distributed by:

AUSTRIA	HELMUTH FELDER Verlag und Buchhandel Karmelitergasse 10 – A - 6020 Innsbruck
BELGIUM	VANDER S.A. – Av. des Volontaires 321 B - 1150 Bruxelles
BRITISH ISLES	PROSVETA Ltd. – 4 St. Helena Terrace Richmond, Surrey TW9 1NR Trade orders to : ELEMENT Books Ltd – Longmead Shaftesbury, Dorset SP7 8PL
CANADA	PROSVETA Inc. – 1565 Montée Masson Duvernay est, Laval, Que. H7E 4P2
FRANCE	Editions PROSVETA S.A. – B.P. 12 83601 Fréjus Cedex
GERMANY	URANIA – Rudolf Diesel Ring 26 D - 8029 Sauerlach
GREECE	PROSVETA HELLAS 90 Bd. Vassileos Constantinou Le Pirée
HOLLAND	MAKLU B.V. – Koninginnelaan 96 NL - 7315 EB Apeldoorn
HONG KONG	HELIOS 31 New Kap Bin Long Village Sai Kung N.T., Hong Kong
IRELAND	PROSVETA IRELAND 24 Bompton Green Castleknock, Dublin
ITALY	PROSVETA – Bastelli 7 I - 43036 Fidenza (Parma)
PORTUGAL	Edições IDADE D'OURO Rua Passos Manuel 20 – 3.° Esq. P - 1100 Lisboa
SPAIN	PROSVETA ESPAÑOLA – Caspe 41 Barcelona – 10
SWITZERLAND	PROSVETA Société Coopérative CH - 1801 Les Monts-de-Corsier
UNITED-STATES	PROSVETA U.S.A. – 3964 Ince Blvd. Culver City, California 90230

Enquiries should be addressed to the nearest distributor

Distributed by:

AUSTRIA HELMUTHER DPR
Verlag und Buchhandel
Kampflinestrasse 10 - A - 6020 Innsbruck

BELGIUM VANDER S.A. - Av. des Volontaires, 321
B - 1150 Bruxelles -

BRITISH ISLES PROSVETA Ltd. - 45L Ghamil Terrace
Richbond, Surr. TW9 4NR
Trade orders to:
ELEMENT Books Ltd - Longmead
Shaftesbury, Dorset SP7 8PL

CANADA PROSVETA Inc. - 1565 Montee Masson
Duvernay, Laval, Que. H7E 4P2

FRANCE Editions PROSVETA S.A. - B.P. 12
83601 Fréjus Cedex

GERMANY URANIA - Rudolf Diesel Ring 26
D - 8029 Sauerlach

GREECE PROSVETA HELLAS
90 Bd. Vassileos Constantinou
Le Pirée

HOLLAND MARTJIR B.V. - Koningslaan 20a 36
NL - 7315 EB Apeldoorn

HONG KONG HELIOS
31 New Kap Bin Long Village
San Kong, N.T., Hong Kong

IRELAND PROSVETA IRELAND
21a Bourpon Green
Coolibrook, Dublin

ITALY PROSVETA
I - 55066 Pakeaza (Roma)

PORTUGAL Edições IDADE DYURO
Rua Passos Manuel 20 - 3°, Esq.
P - 1100 Lisboa

SPAIN PROSVETA ESPAÑOLA - Caspe 41
Barcelona - 10

SWITZERLAND PROSVETA Société Coopérative
CH - 1801 Le Mont-sur-Lausanne

UNITED STATES PROSVETA U.S.A. - 3964 Tivoli Blvd.
Culver City, California 90230

Enquiries should be addressed to the nearest distributor

PRINTED IN FRANCE
NOVEMBER 1984
PROSVETA EDITIONS, FRÉJUS

– N° d'impression : 1380 –
Dépôt légal : Novembre 1984
Printed in France